REFORM OF ENVIRONMENTAL REGULATION

REFORM OF ENVIRONMENTAL REGULATION

WESLEY A. MAGAT
Center for the Study of Business Regulation
Fuqua School of Business
Duke University

BALLINGER PUBLISHING COMPANY
Cambridge, Massachusetts
A Subsidiary of Harper & Row, Publishers, Inc.

iv

International Standard Book Number: 0-88410-908-9

Library of Congress Catalog Card Number: 82-1604

Printed in the United States of America

Library of Congress Cataloging in Publication Data

Main entry under title:

Reform of environmental regulation.

   Includes bibliographical references and index.
   1. Environmental law—United States—Addresses, essays, lectures.
I. Magat, Wesley A.
KF3775.A75R43   344.73'046   82-1604
ISBN 0-88410-908-9   347.30446   AACR2

REFORM OF ENVIRONMENTAL REGULATION

CONTENTS

LIST OF FIGURES

LIST OF TABLES

PREFACE

Early in his presidency Ronald Reagan is attempting to change the
fundamental relationship between our federal government and the
country it serves. Large budget reductions and tax cuts have been
passed, a massive exchange of welfare programs between the federal
government and state governments has been proposed, and regulatory
reform continues to receive steady lip service, if not attention. At a
time in which we are being promised a new relationship between
regulatory agencies, such as the Environmental Protection Agency,
and the firms they discipline and the public they protect, this study of
reform of environmental regulation is particularly appropriate.

Each chapter in the volume, except the first, was commissioned by
the Duke University Center for the Study of Business Regulation for
the Conference on Reform of Environmental Regulation, held at
Duke on May 17 through 19, 1981. The Regulation Center is a faculty
research organization supported by the Fuqua School of Business
and cosponsored by the Economics Department, Institute of Policy
Sciences and Public Affairs, Law School, and School of Forestry and
Environmental Studies. This conference was the third in an annual
series of research conferences on current regulatory problems, with
the first on Regulation and Innovation, the second on Managing the
Transition to Deregulation, and the fourth recently held on Reform
of Banking Regulation.

As organizer of the Conference on Reform of Environmental Regulation, I would like to thank everyone who contributed to its success. In particular, Dean Thomas F. Keller of the Fuqua School of Business provided his generous support for the conference and other Regulation Center activities, Stephanie Frost managed the arrangements almost singlehandedly, the authors provided the new ideas on which the conference was based, and the participants made it come alive.

Wesley A. Magat

1 REFORM OF ENVIRONMENTAL REGULATION: AN INTRODUCTION

Wesley A. Magat

The 1980 presidential election and subsequent actions by the Reagan Administration have catapulted regulatory reform to center stage along with taxation and fiscal restraint. The two previous administrations pursued regulatory reform in selected areas, but the current political climate has created the desire and general expectation that our entire regulatory system be restructured. This volume analyzes the important as well as politically and administratively reasonable reforms of one particularly vital set of regulations—those which protect against environmental degradation: We focus on environmental regulation because, among all social regulatory agencies, the Environmental Protection Agency (EPA) probably arouses the most public interest, both through the high compliance costs it imposes upon the private sector, on the one hand, and through the benefits of environmental protection it provides the public, on the other. Closely related to these benefits and costs are the efficiency gains possible from improved EPA regulation, which some analysts believe exceed those of most other agencies. Finally, the various forms that EPA's rules take exemplify most types of social regulation. For example, the Food and Drug Administration's (FDA's) product regulation is similar to EPA's pesticide and toxic substances regulation, and EPA's industrial effluent guidelines are in many ways similar to standards set by the Occupational Safety and Health Administration (OSHA) and the Consumer Product Safety Commission (CPSC).

1

Reform of environmental regulation is a timely subject for several reasons. In 1981 Congress and the administration ducked the scheduled reauthorization of the Clean Air Act, but in 1982 they may well be forced to stand up to the issues; over the last few years EPA has experimented hesitantly with regulatory reform; as a nation we have gained a decade of experience under our major air and water pollution laws; and in the last two decades the academic literature on environmental regulation has grown substantially, slowly working its way into the political system, despite its generally abstract nature. In addition, the recent successes enjoyed by regulatory reform in the traditional areas of economic regulation of airlines, trucks, and railroads has created a momentum for further reform of social regulation, especially of the environment. Perhaps of most relevance, the costs of the 1970s' environmental laws are starting to hit industry hard in a period of stagnant economic growth and depressed profitability. All of these reasons argue that now is the time for careful thinking about the policy options available to improve environmental regulation and about the associated implementation problems, all with a thorough understanding of the institutional and political structure in which that regulation occurs. The following seven chapters contribute importantly to that task.

APPROACHES TO REGULATORY REFORM

In analyzing the range of options for reform of environmental regulation, it is useful to identify five separate approaches: fine-tuning, centralized review, economic incentives, technology basis, and regulatory relief.[1] The first approach of fine-tuning involves adjusting existing programs to ease or eliminate the impacts of the most objectionable parts of legislation and its implementation without changing the basic thrust of the laws. For example, many industrial proponents have argued for piecemeal revisions in the Clean Air Act, most notably, relaxing the stringency of the National Ambient Air Quality Standards, eliminating the Prevention of Significant Deterioration requirements, weakening emission standards for new automobiles, and eliminating New Source Performance Standards (particularly those for coal-fired power plants). Even if this approach is taken, Chapters 3 and 5 explain how most existing forms of environmental regulation could be improved by better risk assessment and policy analysis techniques.

Not all supporters of fine-tuning argue that the basic approaches to air and water pollution control are cost-effective, equitable methods of achieving necessary environmental protection. They recognize that different approaches might be preferable if we could start over, but that we cannot. The existing structure of environmental regulations has developed an extensive set of pollution property rights and has required major capital investments. As Chapter 8 so powerfully explains, any changes in the approach to environmental regulation would cause massive reassignment of those property rights and significant gains and losses in the values of those capital investments. Even if the abatement cost and environmental protection gains from scrapping the existing approaches are worth the costs the changes impose, the political power of groups standing to lose from the changes (or even their uncertainty about being potential losers) might be sufficient to stifle any significant reforms other than through fine-tuning.

Like fine-tuning, the second approach of centralized review is motivated to a large extent by the difficulty of overcoming the tenacity of proponents of existing regulatory forms. Realistically, our current set of environmental laws represents a complex set of political compromises that would require extensive expenditures of time and "political capital" to unravel and reestablish. However, centralized review is a way of redirecting the decisions made by a nonindependent regulatory agency, such as EPA, and avoiding the inevitable congressional battle that would arise over new legislation.

The Office of Management and Budget's (OMB's) Quality of Life Reviews of EPA in the early 1970s and President Reagan's (1981) Executive Order 12291 both took this approach. The Quality of Life Reviews put no substantive requirements on the agency, but it allowed OMB to delay the rulemaking process and to apply pressure on EPA to weaken regulations it felt to be unreasonable. Executive Order 12291 imposes substantive as well as procedural requirements on all nonindependent regulatory agencies, EPA being an important example. Chapter 4 describes the cost-benefit analytical requirements and examines their potential impact on agency decisionmaking. The Executive Order provides OMB with the power to make at least two kinds of reforms in environmental regulations. First, to the extent permitted by varous enabling statutes (an important qualifier), it forces EPA to explicitly consider and use economic efficiency as the major criterion in promulgating standards. Justifying a regulation with a cost-benefit analysis requires measuring benefits as well as costs, and benefits measurement requires improved risk assessment, for which Ware, Vaupel, and Dorfman all suggest improvements. Second, through its procedural requirements the Executive Order allows OMB to hold hostage proposed regulations that do not support other administration goals—from economic problems, such as inflation and budget deficits, to political concerns, such as regulatory cost relief for the steel industry. Thus, centralized review, as implemented by Executive Order 12291, requires significant reordering of the criteria used by EPA in setting standards to give economic efficiency primacy; but it may also allow OMB to shift the emphasis of regulation toward other goals as well.

Economic incentives, the third approach, have already been adopted under EPA's Controlled Trading Program.[2] (See Chapter 6 for a brief history of the program.) The agency's bubble, offset, and banking programs allow firms a limited form of exchange of air pollution rights among sources owned by the same firm or by different firms. These exchange possibilities allow ambient air quality standards to be met more cheaply, and of even more political significance, they allow industrial growth in cities out of compliance with ambient standards, cities that would otherwise find their expansion crimped by existing environmental statutes. More ambitious use of the marketable permits approach would eliminate many of the current EPA restrictions on trades and would directly control the initial distribution of tradable emission permits. Chapter 7, for example, analyzes the problems in implementing a market for sulfates in the Los Angeles Basin.

The use of economic incentives for controlling air and water pollution faces two substantial hurdles. First, beyond the Controlled Trading Program authorized by the 1977 Clean Air Act Amendments, more extensive use of incentive-based approaches would require statutory change before EPA could adopt them, even if the agency wanted to. Any return to Congress opens up a wide range of conflicting interests that make a switch to the economic incentives approach unlikely. Second, the reason for probable congressional inaction is precisely that major wealth transfers would be involved. In Chapter 8, Harrison and Portney explain the nature of the accommodation problems caused by shifting from the current environmental regulation system to one based on economic incentives and identify the likely gainers and losers from the shift.

The fourth approach to environmental regulation is based on a technological approach already incorporated in the air and water discharger New Source Performance Standards and in the water effluent guidelines. Although it is unlikely, Congress could scrap the approach to air pollution control based on National Ambient Air Quality Standards and adopt this technology-based approach in its 1982 reassessment of the Clean Air Act. This approach appears to possess several advantages: if implemented based on accurate engineering data, the discharge standards are technologically feasible to meet; by grouping firms into fairly homogeneous categories, EPA need not set standards for each individual firm; enforcement can be accomplished primarily by checking whether the recommended abatement technology is installed, rather than by more complicated monitoring systems (although there is no assurance that the technology will be operated correctly); new (i.e., unrepresented) firms can be given stricter standards, thereby neutralizing the adverse political consequences of abatement costs (and providing existing firms a competitive cost advantage over new entrants); and uniform national standards eliminate the advantages possessed by firms in less populated and less polluted areas. Despite these seeming advantages over the existing system of air pollution control, several strong disadvantages preclude its adoption. Technology-based standards are grossly inefficient in the sense of failing to minimize the cost of the environmental protection provided, they may reduce abatement innovation because certain existing technologies are locked in, they contribute to restrictions on growth in nonattainment areas because the permits are not tradable, they create "hidden" regional advantages relative to alternative standard-setting procedures, and they tend to focus on end-of-pipe technologies, which may be a more expensive compliance method than process changes.

The final approach has been labeled "regulatory relief" by the Reagan Administration. The name accurately reflects the intent of these regulatory changes, namely, to reduce the costs of compliance. Regulatory relief may, but need not, be consistent with reforms directed at improving the efficiency of regulation, such as Executive Order 12291. If the relief is granted to the firms facing the highest compliance costs (per unit of waste), then it also promotes more cost-effective regulation. Fortunately, the industrial sectors with the strongest political claims for relief may also be facing the highest compliance costs, in which case more efficient regulations would tend to result. But even if more cost-effective regulations are produced, the level of environmental quality will tend to be reduced.

Harrison and Portney's analysis of the transition problems created by disgruntled losers in the regulatory reform process helps explain why regulatory relief is more popular than regulatory reform.

Regulatory relief can be provided in four different ways, in order of decreasing effectiveness in providing relief, but unfortunately also in order of increasing ease of implementation. First, Congress can relax regulatory statutes, such as automobile emission requirements. Second, rather than force a congressional decision, EPA can be coaxed through administrative appointments and purposeful oversight to relax existing rules, such as the "best available technology" effluent guidelines. Less effective yet, but easier, the administration can force EPA to slow down or halt the promulgation of new regulations. To the extent that the agency tended to promulgate non-cost-effective standards, the cost-benefit analysis requirements of Executive Order 12291 cause new regulations to be weaker than they would otherwise be. Furthermore, the delay capability of the OMB oversight process can and has slowed down the rate at which major new standards are issued. Finally, to provide relief from existing regulations, the agency, either by its own volition or because of budgetary costs, can reduce its enforcement efforts. To the extent that enforcement efforts, however meager they may have been, induce compliance with existing regulations, we can expect reduced enforcement to result in less compliance and therefore lower abatement costs as well as lower environmental quality.

Why might the administration choose to take the regulatory relief approach, rather than rely solely upon centralized review based on cost-benefit principles, or alternatively rely upon decentralized economic incentive approaches? The administration may be ignorant of the efficiency gains possible through adopting other regulatory approaches, that is, lower aggregate compliance costs and improved environmental quality. But it is more likely that the relief approach satisfies political needs which need not be consistent with more efficient regulation. If the administration were already without the support of the environmental lobby, then alienating them further results in few additional vote losses. Furthermore, an administration providing relief to high abatement cost firms would cause low cost firms that would stand to lose from more efficient regulation to feel betrayed. Also, some forms of regulatory relief, such as reduced enforcement, allow the budgetary requirements of EPA regulation to be reduced, contributing to the solution of another important political problem—namely large budget deficits. An even more sophisticated explanation argues that the administration recognized the political capital it would need to expend to achieve regulatory reform through an approach that yields efficiency gains as well as pure relief. Given a limited supply of this capital and an agenda of tax and fiscal reforms that would draw heavily upon its supply, it may have decided to pursue regulatory relief because other reform approaches would simply be too politically costly.

PREVIEW OF THE CHAPTERS

The following seven chapters each consider one important yet institutionally realistic issue in the reform of environmental regulation. They can be divided conceptually into two groups. The Dorfman, Ware, Freeman, and Vaupel studies all address the problems of developing the scientific data base about environmental hazards, assessing their risks, evaluating those risks and the cost of reducing them, and integrating these tasks into a process that produces the information necessary for a regulator to make informed decisions.

In Chapter 2, "The Lessons of Pesticide Regulation," Dorfman addresses all these problems in the context of a case study. The regulatory management problems of EPA's Office of Pesticide Programs (OPP) are immense. It is charged with controlling the hazards from the use of about 50,000 pesticide formulations that comprise up to 1,800 generic compounds, where the benefits and risks of each pesticide vary across a spectrum of uses. Dorfman identifies the major problems OPP faces in risk assessment and risk evaluation, providing examples of the methods of environmental risk assessment and evaluation suggested in Chapters 3 and 4. He also provides cogent reasons for the usefulness of policy analysis, anticipating the major theme of Chapter 5. Dorfman's suggested reforms of pesticide regulation, some of which are starting to be adopted by EPA, call for a radical revision in our approach to pesticide hazard control and question the usefulness of cost-benefit analysis, as traditionally practiced, in regulating this hazard. His study of this particularly onerous regulatory problem highlights the potential difficulties in synthesizing diverse sources of scientific data about environmental risks, a problem studied generically by Ware.

In Chapter 3, "Health Risk Assessment: The Role of Statistical Analysis," Ware reviews the conceptual and methodological issues involved in health risk assessment and analyzes the problems of using classical statistical methods to assess and report scientific information about environmental health hazards. He suggests the potential desirability of using prior and subjective distributions to synthesize information from different sources about hazards and discusses how to use prior and subjective distributions. Besides offering methodological solutions to some of the risk assessment problems identified by Dorfman, Ware provides an understanding of the accuracy of the benefit estimates which form a key element of the risk evaluation procedures analyzed by Freeman.

In Chapter 4, "Risk Evaluation in Environmental Regulation," Freeman provides guidelines for combining risk and cost assessments in ways useful for making environmental policy decisions, and then applies these guidelines to analyze the likely applications of the cost-benefit analyses required by Executive Order 12291. He distinguishes between two uses of cost-benefit analysis—as a rule for decisionmaking and as a framework for organizing information without dictating a decision—and argues that cost-benefit analysis is extremely valuable in the second role, but often is inappropriate in the first. Consistent with Vaupel's suggestions, Freeman views cost-benefit analysis as a method of reducing complicated information relevant to a regulatory decision to a form useful for decisionmakers, while explaining the logical implications of all major assumptions and why, under different assumptions and different ways of combining the data, the analysis would imply different decisions.

In Chapter 5, "Truth and Consequences: Some Roles for Scientists and Analysts in Environmental Decisionmaking," Vaupel makes two primary contributions to the practice of environmental regulation. First, he explains the proper role of the policy analyst in helping EPA administrators make regulatory decisions, contrasting this role to that of natural scientists and economists. Through caricatures of the narrow perspectives of the natural scientist, economist, and political scientist, he cleverly demonstrates the critical integrative task necessary for policy analysts. Second, Vaupel catalogs three categories of neglected research that could improve the quality of environmental decisionmaking even more than additional scientific research on health effects—research on risk assessment, research on preferences, and research on policy design. Though Dorfman, Ware, and Freeman consider these three areas, Vaupel's integrative approach identifies many further elements of environmental decisionmaking that could be improved through research.

The chapters by Roberts, Hahn and Noll, and Harrison and Portney form the second integrated group of studies in this volume, analyzing the practical problems of implementing an economic incentives approach to regulatory reform (and to a lesser extent the centralized review approach organized around cost-benefit analysis). Roberts concentrates on the problems and solutions of designing and administering EPA's Controlled Trading Program, Hahn and Noll investigate the more ambitious task of designing a market for tradable SO_x emissions permits in the Los Angeles airshed, and Harrison and Portney explain the difficulties of switching from existing approaches to environmental regulation to ones based on economic incentives or cost-benefit analysis. Although there exists an extensive economics literature showing the theoretical desirability of the marketable permits approach to environmental regulation, these three chapters provide the most thorough analysis available of the problems in implementing the approach. As such, they represent an important contribution to the literature and practice of environmental regulation.

In Chapter 6 "Some Problems of Implementing Marketable Pollution Rights Schemes: The Case of the Clean Air Act," Roberts argues persuasively that no marketable permits scheme, no matter how finely tuned, can achieve all the benefits associated with the textbook versions of that approach because the more fine-tuned the scheme, the greater the associated transactions and knowledge costs. He illustrates this thesis by explaining the many problems that have arisen in implementing EPA's Controlled Trading Program: the unreliability of pollution monitoring (although not just a problem for incentives approaches); the proper scope of pollution to count in trades (e.g., air pollution caused by ships delivering raw materials to a plant); the comparability of new and existing sources of pollution by location and by time of discharge; market thinness; the lack of well-defined existing pollution rights; and the fact that transactions are not self-policing. After offering suggestions for ameliorating these problems, he concludes that the difficulty of implementing marketable permits schemes will usually be significant and will depend upon technical features of each market; but if these problems are borne in mind, the approach can be quite attractive.

Hahn and Noll examine the implementation of a more extensive permits market in Chapter 7, "Designing a Market for Tradable Emissions Permits," asking how to design a successful market for SO_x permits in California's South Coast Basin. After estimating the abatement cost functions of major polluters in the region, they determine (for four possible ambient air quality standards) the expected price of permits, annual abatement costs, annual cost savings from more efficient control, and the market value of the permits. Neither of two potential problems they identify—market power and "hot spots"—are significant for the Los Angeles market, yet they could be in other areas for other pollutants. A third major problem, that of the initial allocation of permits, will always present a difficult design issue, but Hahn and Noll offer several methods of solving the problem and analyze the likely adverse consequences of each potential solution.

Their study is valuable for several reasons. It demonstrates that implementing a marketable permits scheme for SO_x in the South Coast Basin is likely to work. More important, Hahn and Noll's study suggests that other airsheds can also successfully implement marketable permits systems for SO_x and other pollutants. Although the same level of detailed study may not be necessary before creating pollution rights markets elsewhere, they provide a methodology for those studies and an outline of the critical design issues to resolve.

If economic incentive schemes or other reforms are ever to be adopted, not only must they be shown to be feasible, but we must learn how to make the transition from existing regulatory approaches. In Chapter 8, "Who Loses from Reform of Environmental Regulation?" Harrison and Portney identify the losers from four categories of economics-based regulatory reform: EPA's Controlled Trading Program, cost-effectiveness tests, cost-benefit tests, and economic incentive schemes. Their list is organized in order of increasing potential efficiency gains, but unfortunately, also in order of the (increasing) number of losers who may need to be compensated. Harrison and Portney suggest and evaluate several ways of accommodating losers, but conclude that the problem is a difficult one. Yet our success in introducing incentive-based reforms may depend critically upon how ingenious we are in accommodating losers, and this chapter provides a thorough analysis of this problem.

FINAL OBSERVATIONS

Although this volume discusses many important issues in the reform of environmental regulation, space constraints cause many others to be left unaddressed. Identifying some of these other reform issues, which will all need attention in the next few years, helps provide a perspective on their broad range. For example, mobile sources contribute the majority of some hazardous pollutants discharged into the air, and mobile source pollution controls pose their own unique set of problems. Much debate has also recently focused on the effects of environmental regulation on industrial innovation. In addition, designing more effective enforcement mechanisms is certainly an important issue for EPA, especially where it must further limit EPA's budget. As another example, new administrations reorganize important agencies, especially when they want to shift the agency's priorities, and the Reagan Administration is no exception. Adopting a better organization structure for EPA might well improve the efficiency of its operations and the quality of its decisions. Finally, improvements in the EPA rulemaking process may lead to beneficial results such as faster promulgation of rules, lower operating costs for the agency and intervenors, less litigation, and rules that better meet the agency's objectives (e.g., protecting the environment, consistency in regulation, process fairness, and rules that promote efficient use of society's resources to protect the nation's environment).

The analyses of the regulatory reform issues in the following chapters are primarily directed toward EPA, but the issues are also of much importance to other social regulatory agencies. The lessons from Dorfman's study of pesticide regulation should also be instructive for FDA; the Ware, Freeman, and Vaupel chapters provide valuable insights about how to produce and transmit scientific information about health hazards and how to assess and evaluate the associated risks, problems of equal importance to OSHA and CPSC; and much of Harrison and Portney's analysis of transition problems applies as well to the implementation of regulatory reforms at other regulatory agencies of the social and economic types.

Reforms of environmental regulation will rank high on the regulatory policy agenda for the next decade, and the seven chapters which follow go far toward explaining how to make that reform truly significant.

NOTES

1. For related discussion, see Harrison and Portney (1981) and Crandall (1981).
2. This program was recently renamed in the Emissions Trading Policy Statement (EPA 1982).

REFERENCES

Crandall, Robert W. 1981. "Has Reagan Dropped the Ball?" *Regulation* 5, no. 5 (September/October): 15—18.

Environmental Protection Agency. 1982. "Emissions Trading Policy Statement: General Principles for Creation, Banking and Use of Emission Reduction Credits." *Federal Register* 47, no. 67 (April 7): 15076–86.

Harrison, David Jr., and Paul R. Portney. 1981. "Making Ready for the Clean Air Act." *Regulation* 5, no. 2 (March/April): 24–31.

Reagan, Ronald. 1981. "Executive Order No. 12291." *Federal Register* 46, no. 33 (February 19): 13193–98.

2 THE LESSONS OF PESTICIDE REGULATION

Robert Dorfman

I want to make it clear from the outset that I have no particular interest in pesticides and no competence in most of the disciplines that have to be employed in studying them. I am not a farmer, agronomist, or horticulturist, nor do I have training in toxicology, oncology, or the chemistry of harmful substances. My own humble crop of tomatoes is harvested every year by some unknown bug rather than by me, and I have about given up the struggle against the magnificent crabgrass that now occupies most of my lawn.

I became involved with pesticides because I wanted to make a case study of some manageable area of environmental regulation that would reveal in concrete form the issues and problems involved. The Environmental Protection Agency (EPA) nominated pesticides so, under the sponsorship of the National Research Council (NRC), I recruited a team that included highly qualified specialists in most of the relevant disciplines. We conducted a detailed review of the kinds of decisions that had to be made and of how EPA is organized to make those decisions. In some instances, we also audited the quality of the resultant decisions.

This paper is based to a large extent on my experience as chairman of the National Research Council Committee on Pesticide Regulation. See National Academy of Sciences, Environmental Studies Board. 1980. *Regulating Pesticides.* Washington, D.C.

A case study of pesticide regulation, of course, is a sample of only one, but I believe that it exemplifies most of the issues and problems that arise in environmental regulation of all types. All of us members of the NRC panel on pesticide regulation, whatever our home disciplines, found the experience instructive and left the committee a good deal wiser than we were when we joined it.

The legal basis for regulation is the Federal Insecticide, Fungicide, and Rodenticide Act of 1947 as substantially amended in 1964, 1975, and later, called by its few friends, FIFRA. FIFRA in its present form requires that all pesticides manufactured or imported for use in the United States be registered by the administrator of EPA, and that the registration must specify, among other things, any limitations on their use. The administrator can decline to register a pesticide if, in his judgment, the hazards of its use outweigh its benefits. He may also place restrictions on its use on the same grounds. In addition, he may suspend or cancel registrations that have already been granted if he learns that they permit chemicals or practices that generate greater hazards than can be justified by their beneficial effects. On top of all that, an amendment passed in 1972 requires the administrator to review the registrations of the some 50,000 pesticides then in use. (About 5,000 new pesticides are proposed for registration every year.) The administrator's responsibilities under this act are discharged through the Office of Pesticide Programs (OPP), which is under the jurisdiction of an assistant administrator for toxic substances and pesticide programs.

CURRENT STATE OF AFFAIRS

The task that a plethora of pesticides (1.6 billion pounds used in nearly 50,000 formulations) and current legislation have set before EPA, and OPP in particular, is awesome. Despite great effort, little progress has been made on this monumental assignment. The current status report indicates that final determinations have been reached on the usability and conditions of use of some fifty pesticides. Thousands still remain on the agenda. It is important to understand why so little has been accomplished.

It must be said that numbers like 50,000 pesticides are scare numbers, useful chiefly for calling attention to a problem. In the first place, these pesticides are compounded out of a much smaller number of active ingredients, variously estimated at 800 to 1800—still an impossible number considering the rate of progress. In the second place, there are no grounds to suspect the safety of many, if not most, of the chemicals utilized—a fact that can be verified without elaborate procedures. This fact has not expedited EPA's progress, however, because the agency has chosen (properly) to turn its attention first to the pesticides about which there are substantial grounds for concern. To understand why the review process is virtually at a standstill, one must understand what is involved in reviewing a pesticide about which there are grounds for suspicion.

EPA responded to the 1972 amendments by establishing a formalized procedure for reviewing the registration of a pesticide. The procedure is called the rebuttable presumption against registration procedure, RPAR for short. The RPAR process begins when a pesticide is placed on the review agenda. Ninety days are then permitted for assembling the requisite data on the risks and benefits associated with that pesticide and for digesting the data. But of course delays may be encountered. At the end of this period, if it appears that there is good cause to deny or limit registration, a notice (RPAR) is published in the *Federal Register*. The applicants for registration, other government agencies, and the general public then have forty-five days in which to submit evidence and briefs in rebuttal of the presumption. Next, the agency considers the responses to the RPAR and, six months after the original publication, is required to issue a document responsive to the registrants' and public's comments, either granting their justness or presenting reasons for refusing to accept them. The packet is then forwarded to the administrator or an assistant administrator for decision. When the decision has been reached, a formal notification of a proposal to regulate is published in the *Federal Register,* together with justifications and supporting documents. Thirty days are then permitted for public comment and thirty more for consideration of these comments before the final decision is reached and published.

In all, the process requires somewhat more than a year if all deadlines are met, which is not to be expected. Some proceedings begun in 1976 are still in progress. Of course, the process can be snarled by lawsuits at any time, even after its completion. The number of years and dollars required to process a single pesticide is considerable. Clearly, handling thousands of such processes is out of the question and yet, in every instance, people are involved whose legal rights must be protected.

It should not be imagined that the lengthy process that I have just sketched is devoted entirely to shuffling legal documents. They are merely the visible tip of the iceberg underneath. A great deal of good, hard, and expensive work is done by the agency, the registrants, and the interested public. For instance, the application for registering a new compound must include reports on field trials of its efficacy, on chemical determinations and analyses of its composition and properties, and on laboratory and biological tests of its riskiness. All take time and money. The bill for the biological assay alone typically runs above $250,000. All of the other data required by the RPAR process must be laboriously assembled. EPA is not expected to perform scientific research into the properties and effects of the pesticides that it registers. But it often does perform such research (either in its own laboratories or by contract) long before the procedure begins in order that the requisite data may be available when required.

This brief sketch of the procedure followed in regulating a pesticide should make it clear that it is elaborate, time consuming, and costly. This appears to be inevitable if the safety of the public and the rights of the people concerned are to be protected. But in fact it is so solicitous of the rights of the people concerned that the public safety is not protected, as indicated by the negligible process that has been made in the past half decade toward actually conducting the review of the pesticides in use. The officials at EPA are concerned about this problem, but have not been able to devise a way to expedite the processing.

OPP has not been idle all these years. It is keenly aware of the need to systematize and simplify the procedure and has proposed an approach called generic review, which takes advantage of the fact that all pesticides are based on 1800 or fewer active ingredients. Generic review is not entirely safe since an apparently minor change in molecular structure can make a great deal of difference in effects. But it is a good deal safer than proceeding at the current negligible rate of progress.

All efforts, however, have been frustrated by two great impediments. One is the "pesticide of the month" problem. Perhaps you remember the Kepone disaster in Virginia or the outcry over 2,4,5-T in Oregon. Those are only the most notorious of incidents that occur almost monthly and that require the OPP to divert resources to contending with current emergencies. Since OPP's resources are strictly limited, these frequent diversions, imposed by scare publicity and often enforced by court orders, severely limit its ability to follow a systematic plan of review based on reasoned judgments of the importance and dangerousness of different pesticides.

The other great obstacle, though less irritating, is more fundamental. The regulation of pesticides is analogous to the solution of a huge system of simultaneous equations. The restrictions that are appropriate for any pesticide depend on the availability and effectiveness of substitutes. If, for example, the use of chlorobenzilate is restricted, the farmers can resort to any of three alternative methods of mite control at some increase in cost and a small decrease in effectiveness. What one does not know without investigation is whether or not those alternatives are any less hazardous than chlorobenzilate. Thus the benefits of regulating any one pesticide cannot be assessed without thorough study of a number of others. The same is true of the costs, since the cost of restricting the use of any pesticide is magnified if the best alternatives to it are also restricted. This consideration dictates that whole groups of pesticides should be considered simultaneously, and the members of such a group are not necessarily chemically related.

To summarize the situation thus far, the task of regulating pesticides is so immense that some systematic way to approach the problem is essential, but formidable obstacles stand in the way of devising and implementing one. I turn now to the task of reaching decisions about a particular pesticide once it has arrived at the top of the agenda. As a preface, let me recall the nature of the decision that must be made. Most pesticides are used on a variety of crops by a variety of methods in a number of different geographic regions. A few of them, like DDT and Kepone, are so very hazardous that the law clearly forbids virtually all their uses. Fortunately, few pesticides are so comprehensively hazardous. Consequently, the regulatory decision concerns which uses in which circumstances and in which geographic regions should be allowed. There is therefore a large number of alternatives to be considered rather than a simple yes or no decision. In choosing among these alternatives the risks and the benefits of each have to be compared with those of the others. This can be resolved into the usual three-fold task: estimating the risks entailed by each kind of use of the pesticide, estimating the benefits of each kind of use, and finally comparing the two.

EVALUATION OF RISKS

In practice, the risks that must be taken into account are predominantly risks to the health of both the general public and the people who come into close contact with the pesticide at various stages of its manufacture and use. The menace of primary concern is the danger of inducing cancers or of causing harmful genetic mutations.

EPA is not expected to do any original scientific research in reaching its decisions, but it is expected to be familiar with all the research that has been done that has a bearing on the decision, and to be abreast of the current state of scientific knowledge. Its actual operation on the risk side, then, is to conduct an extensive search of the biological and medical literature and to make a well-reasoned evaluation of the reported findings, which frequently are not consistent with one another. On the other hand, an applicant for registration is required to do a substantial amount of research on the chemical, biological and toxicological properties of the formulation that he wishes to register. The results of the applicant's studies, together with the significant findings from the search of the open literature, form the basis for EPA's estimates of the risks presented by the pesticide in question.

The scientific evidence so acquired is, for all practical purposes, of two sorts: the result of laboratory experiments in which animals are exposed to the pesticide, and epidemiological data on human exposures. In the case of pesticides, epidemiological data are rare and often unsatisfactory. It is easy to see why. New pesticides must be registered before there is any human exposure. For pesticides, there is rarely a record of the extent of exposure and when there is, it is impossible to relate exposure to effects except in the most dramatic instances. This is because carcinogenic and mutagenic effects are typically latent for many years after initial exposure.

Primary reliance, therefore, is placed on the results of animal experiments, but these too are fraught with difficulties. Two difficulties figure especially large in the literature. One is the problem of extrapolating from laboratory animals to human beings. It is frequently asserted that every substance that is carcinogenic in men is also carcinogenic in some animal species. But that is not at issue. The issue is whether or not people can safely be exposed to a substance that has been found to induce malignancies in laboratory animals, or, for that matter, has not been found to do so. This is very tricky. For example, chlorobenzilate has been found to induce tumors, possibly malignant, in male mice but not in female mice and not in rats. Experienced oncologists are not surprised by such selectivity. It is believed that slight differences in the hormonal content of an organism's blood make great differences in its defenses against tumors. This fact makes it perilous to draw inferences from animal experiments though they remain the best indicator we have.

The other difficulty is a different kind of extrapolation. If a pesticide is used, people will be exposed to doses of one or two micrograms a day, and we should regard a substance as dangerous if such a dose induced cancers in perhaps one in a hundred thousand or one in a million of the people so exposed. To detect such tiny probabilities would require experiments in which at least 300,000 animals were exposed to the substance in question, even if there were no background exposure. Such large-scale experiments are out of the question. So in order to attain a probability of inducing cancer that is high enough to be observed in a reasonable sample, enormous doses are given. Typically these doses are several thousand times as great as the doses human populations are expected to experience. Thus arises the problem of how to infer from responses to gigantic doses what the responses to the tiny doses likely to be experienced in practice will be. There seems to be no generally accepted solution.

These are not the only problems with using laboratory experiments to decide whether pesticides or other substances are dangerously carcinogenic. The conduct and evaluation of laboratory experiments are more complex than a nonbiologist would expect. Several hundred animals must be kept alive for more than a year. When any animal dies, and some always do, an autopsy is required to determine whether the death is attributable to the substance being studied. If there should be a contagion—and contagions do occur with laboratory animals just as they do with any living things confined together in a small space—all is lost. At the end of the experiment, each surviving animal is sacrificed. Slides are made of a sample of its tissues and examined for detection of tumors. The interpretation of the slides is so delicate that pathologists often disagree in their interpretations. In short, the conduct of laboratory experiments introduces considerable random error even when the number of animals in the sample is large. Moreover, we are frequently concerned not with a single substance but with comparing the carcinogenic potencies of several substances, for example, a particular pesticide and its alternatives. In such cases, the importance of the various sources of estimation and measurement error is magnified.

To go further, suppose that we had a good and decisive laboratory experiment, a reliable method for extrapolating from animals to people, and a way to extrapolate from high doses to low ones. We should still need estimates of the number of people who would be exposed to different doses and for different periods of time. The people who manufacture, apply, and otherwise handle the pesticide are few, but they are relatively highly exposed. The people who ingest the foods treated with the pesticides are numerous, but they are only slightly exposed. If aerial spraying is used or if rain washes some of the pesticide into public waters, still other population groups are exposed.

There may be many distinguishable population groups, and for each of them the number of the people in the group and the dose that each member is likely to receive should be estimated. The largest group is generally the people who eat the foods treated with pesticide. To estimate the dose that each member of that group might receive, one must estimate, for example, how many people eat, let us say, oranges. One must also estimate how much of the pesticide residue remains on the food at the time it is harvested and how much survives the processing, handling, and cooking that intervenes between the harvest and the ultimate consumption. Consider chlorobenzilate again. It is used on oranges, and the residue remains on the skin of the orange rather than penetrating it. Unless one sucks the orange without washing it thoroughly, one is not likely to receive any of the pesticide. Nor will one receive any by drinking frozen orange juice made from treated fruits. But the skins of the oranges used in freezing plants and by other processers are ground up and used in cattle feed. Thus, people other than vegetarians may ingest chlorobenzilate by that indirect route. Other pesticides are transmitted to people by other routes. In general, so much depends on eating habits and methods of preparation that it is not easy to estimate either the number of people exposed or the amounts to which they are exposed.

So ends my catalogue of the difficulties to be surmounted in assessing the risks imposed by the use of any pesticide. It is a discouraging catalogue. What we should like to obtain as a result of investigation are estimates of the number of people who are likely to contract cancer from exposure to a pesticide when it is used in accordance with any of the available regulatory options. These estimates, if available, would be basic ingredients for making a choice among the alternatives. EPA tries to make those estimates and, indeed, routinely produces figures that purport to convey the desired information. Having inspected a number of such estimates and the methods used to derive them, I believe this practice is misleading and imparts an unwarranted impression of scientific certitude. This opinion is fairly widely shared. The report of the Work Group on Risk Assessment (1979:77) of the Interagency Regulatory Liaison Group asserts: "Given the present state of knowledge, the quantitative assessment of cancer risks provides only a rough estimate of the magnitude of the cancer risks which may be useful in setting priorities among carcinogens and in obtaining a very rough idea of the magnitude of the public health problem posed by a given carcinogen." In other passages it urges extreme caution in using numerical risk estimates for regulatory purposes, and there is much more testimony to the same effect.

The recommendation of the NRC committee on pesticides was to be candid about the limitations of scientific knowledge and to abstain from making extrapolations and estimates for which no sound scientific basis exists. This means, in effect, presenting the results of the laboratory experiments and any other hard data, but not indulging in any guesswork. We felt that the guesswork and the exercise of judgment for which science provides little or no foundation belongs in the province of the administrator and his senior staff, and that scientists and subordinate staff should not substitute their judgments for those of responsible officials.

EVALUATION OF BENEFITS

We turn now to the second major task to be performed in deciding on a regulation, namely, estimating the benefits of using the pesticide. In this context, the word benefits always means the benefits of using the pesticide without regulation as compared with those of using it in accordance with a proposed regulatory restriction—in other words, the benefits foregone by imposing the restriction. The task of estimating these benefits is entirely standard, so I do not have to devote much time to it.

Conceptually, the analysis of benefits rests on the notions of consumers' and producers' surpluses. For each crop on which a pesticide is used there is a demand curve and also a supply curve for each of the regulatory options that might be adopted. Concentrate for the moment on the supply curve corresponding to unregulated use of the pesticide. The point where this supply curve cuts the demand curve marks the equilibrium price and quantity under unregulated conditions. If we imagine a horizontal line drawn at the level of the equilibrium price, the area between it and the demand curve is the consumers' surplus under unregulated conditions. Similarly, the area between the horizontal line and the supply curve is the producers' surplus, and the sum of these two areas is the total social surplus from the unregulated use of the pesticide.

The effect of imposing any regulation is to raise the supply curve, which will then intercept the demand curve at a higher equilibrium price and a lower equilibrium quantity. The consumers' surplus will thereby be reduced and the producers' surplus will usually be reduced also. In some circumstances, though, the increase in price will actually increase the producers' surplus but never by enough to offset entirely the shrinkage in consumers' surplus. Thus the total social surplus will always be reduced. This decrease in the total social benefits is then the social cost of that regulatory alternative.

There is no special difficulty about estimating the demand curves. In fact, they can frequently be taken directly from marketing studies made by the Department of Agriculture. The supply curves do present some problems, for they cannot be observed directly for a number of reasons. One reason is that most agricultural products are not exchanged in freely fluctuating, competitive markets. The supply of many agricultural products is controlled by marketing orders that prevent production from expanding to the point where marginal cost is equal to price. Other agricultural products are subject to other types of output restriction designed to prevent excessive production at the established support price. In these cases, observed market behavior will not reflect the competitive response of supply to price changes.

Besides, most of the supply curves required are hypothetical, that is, they are estimates of the supply that would be forthcoming under various restrictions on the use of pesticides that have not, in fact, been experienced. As a result, the supply curves must be inferred by estimating the marginal cost curves that would correspond to the different alternative regulations under consideration. I have already mentioned that these marginal cost curves require making assumptions about the methods of pest control to which farmers would resort if use of the pesticide in question were restricted. Neither the demand curves nor these marginal cost curves can be estimated with any great precision, but they do not present any peculiar difficulties.

In actual practice, the methods of benefit estimation used by EPA are not even this elaborate. Their standard method is simply to estimate the increase in farm costs per unit of output imposed by a regulation under evaluation and to multiply this by the forecast level of output. Our studies indicate that the error introduced by using this highly simplified procedure can be safely ignored for all practical purposes.

You may have noticed that I have not even mentioned the producers' surplus that accrues to the manufacturers and distributors of the pesticide. This is invariably ignored on the grounds that any reduction in the pesticide manufacturer's profits will be roughly offset by increases in the profits of the manufacturers and distributors of the substitutes that will be used in its place.

The only other aspect of benefit estimation that should be mentioned is the time dimension. The method that I have described is strictly an application of comparative statics and consequently can yield only estimates applicable to a single year. Regulations, however, apply to the use of a pesticide for as long as it will be used if it is permitted or as long as it would have been used if it is banned. With some exceptions, the useful life of a pesticide is not very great. Most become obsolete within ten years of their date of introduction, either because they are superseded by superior formulations or because pests adapt and become immune to them. The cost of regulating a pesticide is therefore the present value, at an appropriate rate of discount, of the costs in each year of its useful life. Those costs will not be uniform but will grow gradually during the early years when it is being introduced and will wane gradually during the later years when it is being phased out. The key difficulty introduced by this consideration is that of forecasting the remaining useful life of a pesticide under review. The cost can be overestimated greatly (as can the risks) by using methods that assume implicitly that the equilibrium corresponding to any regulatory alternative will persist indefinitely.

EVALUATION OF THE OPTIONS

The third major task is to choose the preferred regulatory option in light of the estimates of risks and benefits just described. This is the payoff task and is probably the hardest one of all.

The officials responsible for the decision would like to be provided with estimates of the risks resulting from each option, reduced to monetary terms. These could easily be compared with the estimates of the monetary benefits foregone, and reaching a decision would require little more than subtracting the cost of each option from the value of the risks that it avoids and selecting the option for which the net benefits are greatest. We have already seen several reasons why this cannot easily be done. In addition to the difficulties already reviewed, reducing to monetary terms risks to life and health introduces yet another unsolvable problem: that of assigning explicit monetary values to changes in the probabilities of illness and death. I do not have to dilate upon that familiar problem. These difficulties notwithstanding, EPA's current evaluation procedures call for expressing the risks of alternatives in just those terms. I do not think, however, that the estimates made receive any more credence than they deserve.

Our review of the difficulties of risk estimation has shown that the goal of arriving at monetary estimates of the benefits and costs of a pesticide regulation, which can be compared directly, is more demanding than can be achieved. As much as that achievement would facilitate making regulatory decisions, we have to confront the fact that choosing among regulatory alternatives is a problem in multiobjective decisionmaking. At the simplest, two considerations have to be weighed: the economic costs imposed by a proposed regulation, and the resultant risks to public health. Furthermore, there is generally no reliable way to express those risks in terms of socially meaningful magnitudes such as the probable effect of the regulation on the incidence of cancers. In practice, the most that EPA can control is the amount of a pesticide discharged into different segments of the environment. How many people will then be exposed to the pesticide, how large a dose each will receive, and how many will suffer ill effects are questions to which we have no well-founded answers.

Responsible officials are then presented with impossible questions such as: Is it worthwhile to forego $5 million a year in economic benefits in order to reduce the amount of heptachlor to which a group of ten million people is exposed from an average of 0.6 to 0.4 milligrams per lifetime? The only way that I can answer such a question is to invoke another tenuous form of extrapolation. For example, we have persuasive epidemiological evidence that 2,4,5-T induces spontaneous abortions in people as well as in rats. Therefore, the finding that another pesticide is as effective an abortifacient as 2,4,5-T under laboratory conditions is fair prima facie evidence that that pesticide is unfit for unrestricted use, particularly if it is related chemically to 2,4,5-T. In general terms, the laboratory behavior of substances for which we have confirmatory evidence, epidemiological or other, can be used to calibrate and interpret the results of laboratory tests of chemicals for which there is no outside evidence. This does not make difficult decisions easy, and officials responsible for making regulatory decisions do not welcome the burdens that using such comparative data place on them.

The real decision problem is actually worse than I have portrayed it. We do not know, in fact, what the foregone benefits from any regulatory option will be. All that is available is an estimate known to be subject to a wide margin of error. For comparison with that imprecise estimate, we have an estimate of the amount of a chemical to which people will be exposed that is at least as imprecise, and impressions about the effects of those exposures that are even more vague. Thus, the estimates presented to the officials are merely sample points surrounded by billowing clouds of uncertainty. Furthermore, we have already noted that the alternatives to be compared rarely involve single population groups, which means that an alternative that reduces the amounts to which one group is exposed may increase the dosages received by one or more others. Furthermore, although effects on health are invariably the primary consideration, effects on wildlife and on ecological stability are often severe enough to be significant components of the benefits of restricting the use of a pesticide.

In short, there is nothing peculiar about the ultimate choice of an alternative for regulating a pesticide. It is a tough regulatory decision in which the administrator, subject to very general legislative guidance, must use his judgment to choose among alternatives whose consequences for good and ill differ in a number of incommensurable ways and are only vaguely foreseeable. The staff work that I have been describing tries to lighten this burden, but cannot make it very light. It assists the administrator by assembling a wide range of relevant data and using the relevant scientific disciplines to interpret them. The result is a characterization of the probable consequences of each alternative. We can think of it as a matrix with a column for each alternative, a row for each kind of consequence, and, in each cell, an entry that tells the poorest, the best, and perhaps the most probable results to be anticipated if that alternative is adopted. These are the data on which the decision must be based.

Two questions naturally arise: Is that all the guidance that all that data gathering and analysis can provide? And if so, is that elaborate, expensive and time-consuming enterprise worthwhile? I think the answers to both questions are yes. Social decisions inherently amount to judgments in which such facts as are available are brought into contact with perceptions of value that remain inchoate. The analysis helps in two indispensable ways. It informs the decisionmaker of what values are at stake and to what extent. It also systematizes the decision process by providing the decisionmaker with comparable data in a comparable format on each occasion so that it is not necessary for him to resolve the same issues afresh each time he confronts a new pesticide.

WHAT IS TO BE DONE?

Relatively few pesticides whose dangerous effects have been experienced have been regulated. A systematic review of all pesticides in use or proposed for use has been launched, but has been frustrated by formidable obstacles. The present situation is intolerable. The public is not being protected, the law is not being executed, the agency is bogged down in an impracticable task, and the pesticide industry is burdened with oppressive procedural expenses and delays from which only the lawyers benefit.

There are palliatives, some of which have been adopted already. For several years, EPA has been authorized to review the safety of active ingredients and to issue generic registrations for all pesticides that employ ingredients found to meet acceptable generic standards, and it has begun to operate on that more economical principle.

The protracted and highly legalistic procedure necessary before a registration can be denied or restricted is in urgent need of streamlining, although this will entail some weakening of the protections now provided. To require EPA to devote three or four years of effort to restraining the use of a single pesticide, or even family of pesticides, effectively prevents it from proceeding expeditiously through the long list of chemicals that await inspection. If Congress is serious about its intention that EPA review all pesticides in a reasonable period of time, then it must admit the possibility of mistakes and allow EPA to arrive at decisions with less documentation and review than is now required of it. On the one hand, the administrator should be allowed to rely on short term tests of carcinogenicity, such as the Ames Test, unless there are substantial indications that a chemical is dangerous. On the other hand, when the administrator finds that the use of a pesticide imposes excessive risks in relation to its benefits, he should be authorized to deny that use, and the applicants should be required to assume a heavy burden of proof in any review or appeal from his decision.

The procedure for selecting the chemicals to be reviewed each year should be systematized and simplified. The National Cancer Institute has adopted a useful procedure. They rely on a panel of experts, mostly from outside the institute, which nominates a short list of substances for early attention using little more information than their collective wisdom, and taking into account both the strength of the indications of dangerousness and the practical importance of a chemical as inferred from the extent to which it is likely to be used. EPA should establish such an agenda panel to select pesticides for early review. The panel should use the two criteria adopted by the NCI, plus a third. Since it is difficult to make reasoned decisions about a pesticide if the alternatives to it have not been reviewed, when a chemical is placed on the agenda for early review it should be accompanied by its close substitutes if at all possible. Deviations from the selections of the agenda panel should be rare. Chemicals should be added to their nominations only if there is direct evidence that they are harmful to humans in the dosages normally experienced.

The procedure for estimating risks is in need of simplification. The current procedure is pretentious, and requires much more work and time than the reliability of the results can justify. No more should be attempted than to place a suspect pesticide in one of four or five risk classes, ranging from substances that are known to be highly toxic to those for which no evidence of harmfulness is found. The regulatory decision for any particular pesticide would then resolve into a judgment as to how great the benefits must be in order to justify exposing the estimated number of people to a substance that is located in its risk class. If structured in this way, the difficult regulatory judgments would be greatly facilitated and could be routinized as precedents accumulate.

The foregoing suggestions are merely stopgaps intended to render an unwieldy task more manageable. They do not attack the fundamental problem, which is that in the present state of understanding, the only way to ascertain whether or not a chemical is dangerous is to try it out. The available methods for trying a chemical are inordinately expensive and time consuming, and produce results that are far from decisive. Using such methods to inspect thousands of chemicals one-by-one constitutes a task that will extend beyond any reasonable time horizon and will cost hundreds of millions of dollars. The only real solutions are either to devise a quick and simple test that is reasonably reliable or, even better, to learn how to predict from a chemical's formula how it will act in the human body. I suppose that a Nobel Prize is waiting for any organic chemist or molecular biologist who makes substantial progress in either of those directions. Certainly, it is of primary importance that EPA actively stimulate and support the basic research that must be performed before thousands of new pesticides and other toxic substances can safely be broadcast throughout the environment.

Those critical scientific breakthroughs appear to be far off. Meanwhile, we must manage. How? An economist's thoughts turn naturally to economic expedients. The one that I shall suggest follows from my previous suggestion that pesticides be classified into risk classes based upon judgmental assessment of the available evidence about them. The notion is to assess fees on the use of pesticides according to the risk classes in which the pesticides are located. The highest risk class should be reserved for pesticides that have been demonstrated to be so risky that no conceivable benefits would justify exposing any substantial population to their effects. Any member of this class should be strictly forbidden. The fee for pesticides in the next highest risk class should be high enough to preclude their use in all but the most urgent circumstances. And so on down the line to the lowest risk class, for which no fee should be charged. It would then be the user's decision whether or not the benefits of a pesticide in a high risk class were great enough to outweigh the social costs as indicated to him by the fee that he would be required to pay. Thus the present detailed evaluation of the benefits and costs of regulatory alternatives would become otiose.

The administrative problems of the plan described above would be minimal since the fees could be collected at the manufacturing level. There is one great difficulty, but it is a concentrated one. Four or five fees would have to be established, and these fees would represent those difficult value judgments that I mentioned above. Each one would be, in effect, a judgment of how great an economic benefit our society would be wise to forego in order to spare its members the risks of exposure to the pesticides in a particular class. In principle, there is no formula that can produce such numbers, and I am sure that many people would be dissatisfied with whatever numbers might be proposed. There is the saving grace that fees could be revised easily from time to time as experience accumulates. But there are surely more difficulties that have not occurred to me. At the moment, I am not prepared to advocate this device though I do recommend it as worthy of study.

I said at the outset that I am not particularly interested in pesticides, though in the course of this study I came to understand much about their importance and the importance of their dangers. I undertook the work in order to learn about the problems that arise in using regulatory methods to protect the environment and to promote other social ends. My study and discussion of pesticide regulation are intended to apply much more broadly. As far as I can make out, pesticides are an entirely typical instance of regulatory problems. The efforts of EPA and the other regulatory agencies are confounded repeatedly by lack of fundamental understanding of the mechanisms they are charged with controlling, by the need to resort to awkward and unsatisfactory expedients to establish their regulations, and by the interminable litigation to which these circumstances give rise. All of the protective legislation that I know of encounters obstacles that are identical in principle to the ones that arise in regulating pesticides. The lessons that emerge from the instance of pesticides are thus widely applicable.

REFERENCES

Work Group on Risk Assessment. 1979. "Scientific Bases for Identifying Potential Carcinogens and Estimating their Risks." Report to the Interagency Regulatory Liaison Group, Executive Office of the President (February).

3 HEALTH RISK ASSESSMENT: THE ROLE OF STATISTICAL ANALYSIS

James H. Ware

Many problems of environmental regulation involve complicated tradeoffs between health, economic, and social consequences. These consequences may be substantial while the relevant information is extensive, incomplete, and poorly organized. Thus, a thorough analysis of regulatory decisions is frequently justified.

In Chapter 5, Vaupel describes the decomposition of regulatory decisionmaking into a set of specialized tasks. One of these tasks is *health risk assessment*—the elicitation, evaluation, and synthesis of the information about the health effects of the environmental hazard under consideration. The goal of assessment is estimation of the probabilities (risks) and magnitude of adverse health effects associated with alternative regulatory policies. This chapter reviews some of the conceptual and methodological issues that arise in health risk assessment. We argue that the statistical methods commonly used in analyzing and reporting scientific information are poorly suited to this task, and discuss the role of prior and subjective distributions in synthesizing information from different sources.

This discussion is heavily influenced by recent work with colleagues to assess the health effects of atmospheric sulfur oxides (SO_x)

This work was supported in part by grant ES01108-08 from the National Institute of Environmental Health Sciences and by grant RP-1001 from the Electric Power Research Institute.

and particulate matter (PM) (Ware et al. 1981), and begins with a description of that problem. The methodological issues described here arise in assessing the health effects of other potentially toxic substances as well. Dorfman discusses some of the same issues in the context of pesticide regulation elsewhere in this volume. However, there may be important differences between the assessment problem for air pollutants and other toxic substances and that for catastrophic events, such as a nuclear accident or dam failure.

THE PROBLEM

Sulfur oxide and particulate air pollution is a problem of international importance. Because these pollutants arise in large part from the combustion of fossil fuels, most of the U.S. population is exposed to ambient sulfur oxides and particulate matter in concentrations that may affect health. The Clean Air Act Amendments of 1970 and 1977 require the Environmental Protection Agency (EPA) to set primary National Ambient Air Quality Standards (NAAQS) "the attainment and maintenance of which . . . is requisite to protect the public health."[1] The EPA is required to document the scientific basis for the standards in air quality criteria documents. Further,

> In setting such air quality standards, the [administrator] should consider and incorporate not only the results of the research summarized in the air quality criteria documents, but also the need for margins of safety. Margins of safety are essential to any health related environmental standards if a reasonable degree of protection is to be provided against hazards which research has not identified (Senate Committee on Public Works 1974).

Although the Clean Air Act prohibits consideration of the economic consequences of NAAQS, the potential economic effects of strict emission standards for power plants, steel mills, and other heavy industries are enormous.

EPA (1981) has recently distributed the second draft of the air quality criteria document for SO_x and PM. It summarizes the scientific evidence concerning respiratory health effects of SO_x and PM. These effects may include transient and permanent reductions in lung function and capacity, cough, wheeze, transient respiratory illness, bronchitis, emphysema, and death. The document also considers effects on welfare such as visibility, damage to vegetation, and impact on lakes, but we exclude these effects and their implications for secondary NAAQS.

The scientific evidence regarding respiratory health effects of sulfur dioxide (SO_2) and PM comes from animal, occupational, clinical, and population studies. Professor Dorfman has described the limitations of animal studies, especially the uncertainties of extrapolating their results to man. However, epidemiological studies also have major limitations. Occupational studies are questioned because working populations are frequently selected to exclude sensitive individuals and because occupational exposures are both different from and greater than ambient air pollution. Thus, population epidemiological studies have a natural appeal because they are directly relevant.

Unfortunately, these studies are also subject to important uncertainties:

1. The health effects of SO_2 and PM are probably small relative to the effects of smoking and individual variability arising from lifestyle, genetic background, occupation, and other factors.
2. The actual exposure burden of individuals in studied populations varies considerably around the concentrations measured at outdoor stations (Melia et al. 1981; Dockery and Spengler 1981). The methods used for outdoor monitoring have also changed rapidly over recent years and studies have used several different methods for measuring PM pollution.
3. Reports of respiratory illness from self-completed questionnaires are subject to errors of recall and medical misconceptions.

Despite these shortcomings, epidemiological studies have been accepted in most assessments as the most useful information for quantifying the risk of exposure to SO_2 and PM (Ware et al. 1981; EPA 1981; Bennett et al. 1979).

Most studies of the health effects of air pollution can be considered either investigations of *acute* health effects—those that occur within minutes or hours of exposure to elevated concentrations of air pollutants—or of *chronic* health effects—those that develop over years of exposure to modestly elevated concentrations. This distinction is reflected in the current NAAQS, which include standards for both the 24-hour and annual average concentrations of SO_2 and total suspended particulate matter (TSP). In this chapter, we consider a single health outcome, persistent cough, and its association with chronic exposure to elevated concentrations of particulate matter. This permits a careful discussion of the methodological issues that arise in combining evidence without a lengthy discussion of an extensive and complex scientific data base.

To assess the public health burden of increased prevalence of persistent cough associated with exposure to particulate air pollution, we need two inputs:

1. An estimate of the exposure-response function quantifying the expected prevalence of persistent cough at different concentrations of TSP or any other measure of particulate pollution.
2. The estimated distribution of exposure now and under alternative regulatory strategies.

A comprehensive assessment of the respiratory health effects of sulfure oxides and particulate matter would require simultaneous estimation of the exposure-response functions for persistent cough and all other indexes of respiratory morbidity and mortality for each pollutant. We first consider the inference problem for a single health effect and then assess the larger problem of synthesizing evidence for several health effects.

Suppose, then, that y is a health effect that is either present or absent in an individual. The exposure-response function in a specified population can be expressed as

$$P(y \text{ present}|x),$$

the probability that y is present in a randomly selected member of the population exposed to concentration x of the pollutant. Suppose also that the exposure in that population is characterized by a probability distribution function, $h(x)$. Then the expected prevalence of y in the exposed population is

$$E(y) = \int_- P(y \text{ present}|x)h(x)dx. \qquad (3-1)$$

Uncertainties associated with estimation of $P(y \text{ present}|x)$ and $h(x)$ will result in uncertainty about $E(y)$. The next section discusses methods for estimating these functions. Before turning to that task, however, we will briefly describe part of the epidemiological evidence and indicate some of the important sources of uncertainty in an assessment.

Chronic Exposure and Persistent Cough

We have noted that a variety of respiratory health effects may result from exposure to high concentrations of SO_2 and PM. We focus here on the evidence for increased prevalence of persistent cough in association with exposure to high concentrations of air pollutants, and its implications for public health. A number of studies have examined the association between persistent cough and air pollution concentration by comparing prevalence rates in communities with large differences in air quality. There is considerable disagreement in the scientific community about the relative validity of various studies, but studies by Lunn et al. (1967, 1970), Lambert and Reid (1970), and Rudnik (1977) are frequently cited. These studies compared prevalence rates in four groups of children, four groups of adults, and three groups of children, respectively. These prevalence rates are shown in Figures 3-1, 3-2, and 3-3 plotted against annual mean concentrations of Black Smoke (BS), the measure of particulate pollution most frequently used in European studies.

Figure 3-1.   Prevalence of Frequent Cough among Children by Concentration of Black Smoke in Four Communities Studied by Lunn et al. (1967, 1970).

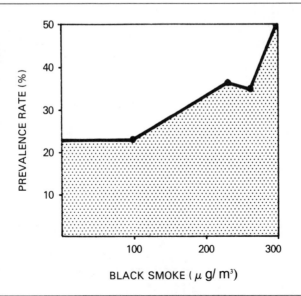

Figure 3-2. Prevalence of Persistent Cough and Phlegm among Adults by Concentration of Black Smoke for Four Groups Studied by Lambert and Reid (1970).

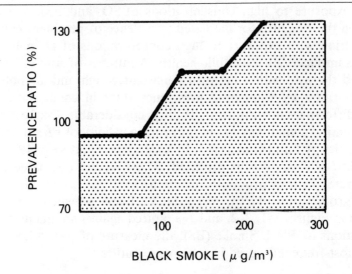

Figure 3-3. Prevalence of Chronic Cough among Children by Concentration of Black Smoke in Three Areas Studied by Rudnik (1977).

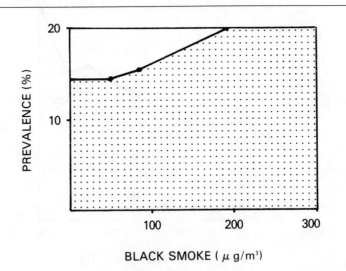

Concentrations of SO_2 were also measured in these three studies. Figure 3-4 shows the annual mean concentrations of SO_2 plotted against the annual mean concentrations of BS in two of these studies. (The data were not available in this form for the third.) The'high collinearity ($r = 0.94$) suggests that the effects of SO_2 and PM will not be separable in these studies.

What are the major sources of uncertainty in using these studies as a basis for choosing the NAAQS? One is sampling variability, the variation in observed rates among random samples chosen independently from the same population. A second is confounding, the variation arising from systematic differences between groups in other characteristics associated with respiratory illness. Possible candidates for confounding variables include individual or family smoking habits, indoor air pollution, crowding and other conditions of living, and, among adults, occupational exposure. Each of these studies had some information on smoking habits and socioeconomic status, and examined the associations between the prevalence of cough and these

Figure 3-4. Sulfur Dioxide and Black Smoke Concentration in Four Areas Studied by Lunn et al. (1967, 1970) and Four Areas Studied by Rudnik (1977).

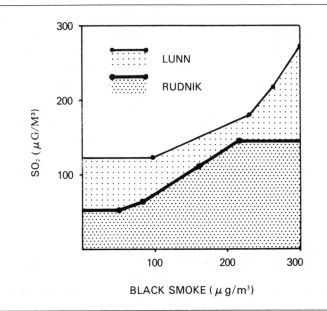

variables. However, we recognize that these variables are inevitably imperfectly defined and may fail to correct adequately for confounding. Often, communities with high and low air pollution concentrations differ in important ways that are difficult to quantify. A dramatic example arises in the comparison of an urban area with a farming community.

The third major source of uncertainty arises from the limitations of air pollution measurements. We assume for simplicity that all measurements were accurately gathered at outdoor stations. (This is rarely true historically.) The exposures of individuals may differ substantially from those concentrations. Evidence from studies of indoor and outdoor pollution and from personal exposure studies suggests that personal exposures in different communities may be more similar than outdoor measurements would suggest. Furthermore, these studies used BS as the measure of particulate concentration, while current NAAQS are based on TSP concentrations. Some experts believe that concentrations of TSP cannot be reliably estimated from reported BS concentrations, and that these studies do not provide a basis for assessing the health effects of PM pollution measured in units of TSP. To complicate matters further, we are uncertain about the proper metric for quantifying air pollution exposure. Although we often use annual mean concentration, the peak exposures may be more important than this metric suggests. The problem is minimized by the high collinearity of different percentiles of the exposure distribution across sites and time. However, it is an important consideration both in evaluating evidence and choosing a regulatory strategy.

These are some, but not all, of the important uncertainties. We have deliberately simplified the problem to the estimation of the exposure-response function for a single health effect. We have chosen three studies and set aside others that might have been considered. We have also set aside the problem of estimating individual exposure. We turn now to a discussion of this simplified estimation problem, anticipating that the major issues can be developed and then applied in a wider context.

STATISTICAL METHODS FOR RISK ASSESSMENT

At least three basic methods have been used to summarize evidence. The first is based upon the frequentist view of statistics and considers the behavior of independent samples from the same population. This approach to statistical inference leads to confidence intervals and significance tests for the parameters of interest, and is the method ordinarily used for reporting evidence in the biomedical literature. A second approach is based upon Bayesian methods. Here, the role of the prior distribution summarizing the knowledge about parameters of interest *prior* to data collection is emphasized. A third approach related to Bayesian methods is the elicitation of subjective probability distributions summarizing the beliefs of expert assessors. The concept of subjective probability provides a framework for eliciting and reporting the assessments of individual scientific experts. These subjective probability distributions may be directly obtained without explicit discussion of the scientific data base. Although a detailed comparison of the foundations of these different approaches to inference is beyond the scope of this chapter, we can examine the potential value of each formulation for the task of risk assessment.

Classical Methods

Many biostatisticians and medical scientists are accustomed to using frequentist ideas in reporting scientific evidence. Thus, the medical literature is replete with references to tests of significance, P-values, and confidence intervals. Statisticians have debated the merits of frequentist methods for some time (Birnbaum 1962; Cornfield 1977). We can examine the limitations of these methods for risk assessment by summarizing the evidence described above.

To make some headway, we need a model. This requires strong assumptions. We assume that the relationship between BS concentration and prevalence of persistent cough is linear in the range studied. We ignore differences in the definitions of the endpoint, at least for now, and assume that the concentrations of BS are comparable across studies. Then we perform simple linear regression within each study to estimate the association between changes in BS concentration and the prevalence of cough. We use the logarithm of prevalence as the response variable, so that the regression coefficient will measure the *percentage* increase in prevalence as BS concentration changes. This also allows us to use the prevalence ratios reported by Lambert and Reid without reexpressing them as rates.

The estimated regression coefficients from the three studies are shown in Table 3-1. To combine the evidence, we assume that the three studies represent a sample from a population of studies. We estimate the average value of the slope in this population as the simple average of the three estimates, and the uncertainty of this average by the estimated standard error. This result is also shown in Table 3-1.

The three studies estimate the percentage increase in the prevalence of persistent cough associated with a 10 μg increase in BS concentration to be 3.4 percent, 2.0 percent, and 2.8 percent. The estimates from the three studies are so consistent that it seems useful to note that frequent cough was the first and only endpoint considered in this analysis. Such coherence might not be found for other endpoints. Although the unweighted estimation procedure is somewhat naive, and more sophisticated models based on variance component estimation have been developed (Harville 1977; DuMouchel and Harris 1981), this simplified discussion captures the essence of these methods.

This summary statistic with its standard error has two kinds of shortcomings. First, we have ignored the most important sources of uncertainty, the possibility of confounding, the linerarity assumption, and the quality and relevance of the aerometric data. If we now apply this result to the problem of setting a standard for TSP or some other measure of PM, we introduce uncertainty of conversion and possibly of extrapolation. Since there is no evidence in the studies to quantify these effects, we cannot expect to estimate their impact through data analysis. Second, point estimates and their standard errors are inconvenient for further synopsis. We want to carry this uncertainty about the slope through to estimation of the total health burden after bringing in exposure information. Although we could

Table 3-1. Estimated Regression Coefficients for Three Studies, Their Average, and Its Standard Error.

Study	Coefficient
Lunn et al. (1967, 1970)	0.0034
Lambert and Reid (1970)	0.0020
Rudnik (1977)	0.0028
Average	0.0027
	(0.00035)

accomplish this through sensitivity analysis—considering values of the slope over the range spanned by the confidence interval—we would prefer a more convenient calculus. In the next section, we argue that prior and posterior probability distributions offer a more effective basis for aggregating evidence.

Bayesian ideas.   Continuing with the assumption of a linear exposure-response function, we denote the slope of the function by β. The components of a Bayesian analysis can be simplistically described as the prior distribution, $f(\beta)$, summarizing knowledge about β prior to investigation, the likelihood function, $L(y|x,\beta)$, summarizing the data, and the posterior distribution

$$f(\beta|x,y) \quad = \quad \frac{L(y|x,\beta)f(\beta)}{L(y|x,\beta)f(\beta)d\beta} \cdot \tag{3-2}$$

The posterior distribution summarizes the information about β in a way that is useful for further probability analysis. Probability distributions can be combined with other distributions and with cost inputs to estimate distributions of health effects or of their imputed cost. When we use an improper prior distribution (giving equal weight to every admissable value of β), the posterior distribution is proportional to the likelihood. For instance, if we assume that the estimated slope from each of the three studies is normally distributed with mean β and variance σ^2, we can compute a posterior distribution for β from the three estimates given in Table 3-1. If we estimate σ^2 from the marginal distribution of the least squares estimates (after integrating out β), the estimated posterior distribution of β is normal with mean 0.0027 and variance 1.23×10^{-7}. An elegant example of the use of Bayesian methods in risk assessment is provided in a recent paper of DuMouchel and Harris (1981).

We notice that Bayesian methods, like frequentist analyses, require probability models for the response variable and incorporate data through the likelihood function. We have still not incorporated the uncertainty arising from the linearity assumption, the potential bias, and the conversion of risk to PM measured in TSP units. Although analyses can be imagined that would speak to these issues, at least indirectly, it seems unlikely that we could think of a unified probability model that satisfactorily incorporates each of these uncertainties analytically.

There is, of course, some diffuse information available. Each of these studies has been carefully reviewed, some evidence has been gathered in other studies about concurrent TSP and BS concentrations, and there is also some scanty information about linearity, perhaps even from these studies. However, I believe that conventional statistical methods for summarizing evidence through analyses derived from models are not effective for summarizing such vaguely quantified information. Instead, this kind of uncertainty is best summarized by the subjective probability distributions of experts.

Subjective probability. Several recent papers have argued for the use of subjective probabilities in risk assessment (Richmond 1981), and there is an extensive literature on the elicitation of subjective probability distributions and some of the potential problems (Wallsten and Budescu 1980; Henrion 1981). Here, we focus on the level of disaggregation appropriate for the elicitation.

Consider one extreme. An expert could be asked to estimate the probability distribution of the increased number of early deaths (or the lost years of life) resulting from a relaxation of the NAAQS for TSP to annual means of 100,120,140, and so on. This is still a substantial task of probability elicitation, but we could reasonably expect that a decisionmaker could use a health risk assessment reported in this way from several experts.

These assessments may be dramatically different for different experts. To understand why, we might elicit subjective probability distributions for narrower questions, such as the effect of TSP concentration on the prevalence of cough, or the probable bias in the study of Lunn et al., as well as descriptive information about the credibility of various studies, the impact of relaxed standards on exposure, and other pertinent information. This information would aid the decisionmaker in reconciling discrepancies. Subjective probability distributions could be used along with exposure distributions and imputed values to estimate aggregate health effects. Notice that the elicitation of prior probability distributions for individual studies is not appropriate because the expert has access to all of the information. Similarly, subjective probability distributions for different health effects are dependent.

If several experts provide these distributions and their scientific basis the information can be exchanged and discussed, and the elicitation can be repeated. In principle, the aggregate health effects of changes in NAAQS can be estimated through a series of probabilistic calculations incorporating prior distributions, likelihood, and subjective probability distributions in a mix that is consistent and reflects data availability. In practice, this has the potential to be laborious and confusing. Thus, we need to find a level of disaggregation that provides enough information for the decisionmaker and is also feasible. One attractive model would combine data analysis of the sort we described for studies of persistent cough with elicitation of subjective probabilities. Experts in the health effects of air pollution would begin by reviewing a detailed analysis combining the evidence from available studies. The experts would then report their subjective probability distributions independently. Each might also provide a background document. It would be necessary to obtain joint probability distributions to the extent feasible.

COMBINING PROBABILITY DISTRIBUTIONS

In Equation 3-1, we expressed the expected prevalence of a binary health effect, y, as a function of the exposure-response function, $P(y$ present$|x)$. Suppose that the function is known up to a parameter β. This is analogous to our example in which the exposure-response function was assumed to be linear with slope β. Then we can write

$$E(y|\beta) = \int P(y \text{ present}|x,\beta)h(x)dx$$

to denote the dependence of the prevalence of y on β. If we had a probability distribution for β at hand, obtained subjectively or otherwise, we could compute the expected prevalence of y by integrating over that distribution. For this and other reasons, it would be desirable to aggregate all of the available information into a single probability distribution for β. If these information sources were independent, this could be accomplished in a straightforward way by repeated applications of Bayes rule (Equation 3-2). Typically, they are not independent. Experts ordinarily share a scientific data base, creating dependencies among themselves and with the objective information. Winkler (1981) has recently given a brief review of methods for handling dependencies, most of which are ad hoc, and described a formal solution to the problem when the subjective probability distributions have a bivariate normal distribution. A similar consideration arises in incorporating uncertainty about $h(x)$ in the assessment. Issues such as these, when treated rigorously, lead to a probability calculus that may well be too clumsy to be useful in practice.

DISCUSSION

Although we have argued for the importance of subjective probability distributions as a device for quantifying vague information, most scientists have relatively little experience with reporting or evaluating evidence in this form. It can be difficult to express subjective probabilities, and there are important disincentives to frank reporting of personal probabilities. Many investigators are studying this problem (Tversky and Kahneman 1974; Winkler and Murphy 1976) and we can hope for increasing facility with these ideas. Less is known about the optimal mix between subjective and objective information, how they should be combined, how to handle dependent distributions, and the best level of disaggregation for eliciting expert opinion. These problems involve ideas from the theories of probability and decision analysis, as well as considerations of feasibility. Recall that we have yet to discuss the exposure distribution and the economic and social considerations that will be important to the decisionmaker. Risk assessment and analysis will ultimately require a new language and a way of weighing and synthesizing evidence that allows scientists, decision analysts, and decisionmakers to communicate information about risks. The task for the immediate future is to begin to test some of these ideas and to develop methods that work within the constraints of environmental decisionmaking. It may be useful, for example, to report the views of individual scientific experts in terms of subjective probability distributions. This will sharpen the discussion of disagreements and clarify the communication of assessments to decisionmakers. It may also give analysts greater facility with assessments expressed probabilistically, and make more ambitious attempts at synoptic analysis practicable.

NOTES

1.   Clean Air Act Amendments of 1977, 42 U.S.C., Section 109, 1977.

REFERENCES

Bennett, A.E.; J.R. Cameron; C. du V. Florey; W.W. Holland; J.R. Leeder; R.S.F. Schilling; A.V. Swan; and R.E. Waller. 1979. "Health Effects of Particulate Pollution: Reappraising the Evidence." *American Journal of Epidemiology* 110:525.

Birnbaum, A. 1962. "On the Foundations of Statistical Inference." *Journal of the American Statistical Association* 57:269–306.

Cornfield, J. 1977. "Sequential Trials, Sequential Analysis, and the Likelihood Principle." *American Statistician* 20:18–23.

Dockery, D.W., and J.D. Spengler. 1981. "Personal Exposure to Respirable Particulates and Sulfates." *Journal of the Air Pollution Control Association* 31:153–59.

DuMouchel, W., and J. Harris. 1981. "Bayes and Empirical Bayes Methods for Combining Cancer Experiments in Man and Other Species." Technical Report No. 24, Department of Mathematics, MIT.

Environmental Protection Agency. 1981. *Air Quality Criteria for Sulfur Oxides and Particulate Matter.* Research Triangle Park, N.C.

Harville, D.A. 1977. "Maximum Likelihood Approaches to Variance Component Estimation and to Related Problems." *Journal of the American Statistical Association* 72:320–40.

Henrion, M. 1981. "Assessing Probabilities: A Review." Department of Engineering and Public Policy, Carnegie-Mellon University.

Lambert, P.M., and D.D. Reid. 1970. "Smoking, Air Pollution and Bronchitis in Britain." *Lancet* 1:853–57.

Lunn, J.E.; J. Knowelden; and A.J. Handyside. 1967. "Patterns of Respiratory Illness in Sheffield School Children." *British Journal of Preventive and Social Medicine* 21:7–16.

Lunn, J.E.; J. Knowelden; and J.W. Roe. 1970. "Patterns of Respiratory Illness in Sheffield Junior School Children. A Follow-up Study." *British Journal of Preventive and Social Medicine* 24:223–28.

Melia, R.J.W.; C. du V. Florey; S. Chinn; B.D. Goldstein; A.G.F. Brooks; H.H. John; D. Clark; I.B. Craighead; and X. Webster. 1981. "Indoor Air Pollution and Its Effects on Health." *Royal Society of Health Journal* 101:29–32.

Richmond, H. 1981. *A Proposed Framework for Quantitative Risk Assessment and Decision Analytic Approaches in the Review of National AAQS.* Research Triangle Park, N.C.: Environmental Protection Agency.

Rudnik, J. 1977. *Epidemiologic Study on Long Term Effects on Human Health of Air Pollution.* Prob. Med. Wieku Rozwojowego 7a (Suppl):1.

Senate Committee on Public Works. 1974. *A Legislative History of the Clean Air Act Amendments of 1970, Volume II.*

Tversky, A., and D. Kahneman. 1974. "Judgement under Uncertainty: Heuristics and Biases." *Science* 185:1129–31.

Wallsten, T., and D.V. Budescu. 1980. *Encoding Subjective Probabilities: A Psychological and Psychometric Review.* Research Triangle Park, N.C.: Environmental Protection Agency.

Ware, J.H.; L.A. Thibodeau; F.E. Speizer; S.D. Colome; and B.G. Ferris, Jr. 1981. "Assessment of the Health Effects of Atmospheric Sulphur

Oxides and Particulate Matter: Evidence from Observational Studies." *Environmental Health Perspectives* 41:255-76.

Winkler, R.L. 1981. "Combining Probability Distributions from Independent Information Sources." *Management Science* 27:479-88.

Winkler, R.L., and A.H. Murphy. 1976. "Point and Area Probability Forecasts: Some Experimental Results." *Monthly Weather Review* 104: 86-95.

4 RISK EVALUATION IN ENVIRONMENTAL REGULATION

A. Myrick Freeman III

The administrator of the Environmental Protection Agency (EPA) is by law empowered, and in some cases required, to issue regulations concerning substances whose manufacture, use, and disposal may result in environmental contamination and adverse effects to humans. Decisions about what and how much to regulate have three important characteristics. First, they involve tradeoffs. Second, what is gained and what is given up by regulation are often measured or expressed in different units; that is, they are noncommensurable. Examples include the benefits of reduced risk of ill health and the monetary costs of controlling pollution. Third, benefits and costs are not known with certainty. In particular, there is likely to be uncertainty about the nature of the underlying technical relationships that determine costs and beneficial effects.

This chapter is about risk evaluation, which might be narrowly construed to mean the determination of the value of avoiding a risk of a specified magnitude. But I intend a broader treatment. My subject is how the available information can be organized for decisionmakers faced with choices about regulating substances in the environment.

I would like to acknowledge the helpful comments of Robert C. Anderson, Wesley A. Magat, Henry M. Peskin, and Paul R. Portney on an earlier draft of this chapter. Of course I take responsibility for all opinions and judgments and errors that remain.

47

This information should be organized and presented to clarify the nature of the tradeoffs involved and to enable the decisionmaker to understand and deal with the noncommensurabilities and the uncertainties concerning the magnitudes of risk and cost.

In the next section I briefly review the principles underlying benefit-cost analysis and the information requirements for its successful implementation. I distinguish between the use of benefit-cost analysis as a rule for making decisions and as a framework for organizing information without dictating outcomes. This distinction provides a basis for discussing the wisdom of proposals (or Executive Orders) to require benefit-cost analysis for all environmental regulatory decisions. I then discuss the treatment of uncertainty within the benefit-cost framework. In the third section I review EPA's analysis supporting its regulation of polychlorinated biphenyls. The purpose of the review is to examine the information actually prepared for decisionmakers in EPA in light of the frameworks discussed in the following section. I consider alternative ways in which the information might have been prepared and presented to decisionmakers. The purpose is not to second-guess EPA decisionmakers or to criticize the quality of the data presented to them. Rather, the purpose is to determine whether the way in which the data were presented to decisionmakers enabled them to confront the right issues, to understand the tradeoffs involved, and to appreciate the uncertainties in the data.

FRAMEWORK FOR REGULATORY ANALYSIS

Benefit-Cost Analysis

Benefit-cost analysis refers to a full accounting of all of the beneficial and adverse effects of a proposed action in a common monetary unit, for example, dollars.[1] The economic theory underlying benefit-cost analysis provides a set of definitions and procedures for carrying out the estimation of total benefits and total costs. According to this theory, the monetary values of these effects are computed based upon individuals' preferences.[2] Total benefits and total costs are the sums of the money values placed upon their gains and losses by individuals. Benefit-cost analysis as described here is basically a framework for developing and organizing information. In this sense, benefit-cost analysis is descriptive of the consequences of the policy action. But it is not prescriptive.

Benefit-cost analysis becomes prescriptive if it is coupled with a value judgment that the government should seek to maximize the net benefits of its policy actions. This value judgment turns benefit-cost analysis into a decision rule stating that a policy should be undertaken if its benefits are greater than its costs.[3] Since benefits and costs are summed across all individuals, this value judgment implies that policymakers are indifferent to the way in which benefits and costs are distributed across individuals. A policy with positive net benefits should be undertaken, according to this value judgment, even if the benefits and costs accrue to different groups so that some gain while others lose. The justification for this value judgment is that if net benefits are positive, there is at least the potential for compensation or redistribution such that no one would actually lose. Whether or not compensation should be paid is said to be a value judgment hinging on equity considerations that lie outside the realm of benefit-cost analysis per se.

The following question is often posed: should benefit-cost analysis be required for environmental regulatory decisionmaking? The question is poorly phrased because, as I have indicated, there are two senses in which the term benefit-cost analysis can be used in this context—as a decision rule and as a framework for organizing and presenting information. How one answers the question could easily depend upon which sense of the term one had in mind.

Initially, consider benefit-cost analysis as a decision rule, that is, a requirement that projects be undertaken if and only if their benefits exceed their costs. This requirement was written into the Flood Control Act of 1936 and is now embodied in administration policy in the form of Executive Order 12291 (Reagan 1981). There are three problems with using benefit-cost analysis as a decision rule. The first is one of measurement. There are some types of effects of regulation which in principle can be measured in dollars, but for which the state of the art does not now permit accurate measurement.[4] An example is the value of lifesaving as measured by individuals' willingness to pay for small reductions in the probability of death in a specified time period. This problem might be overcome by devoting substantial resources to measurement efforts. It might also be possible to reach agreement through political means on the shadow prices to be used in valuing certain consequences. But this problem should be confronted before a requirement to base decisions on the outcomes of benefit-cost analysis is established.

The second problem arises when a consequence of a regulatory action is important to decisionmakers, but cannot be valued in monetary terms consistent with the basic principles of welfare economics. Only those things that individuals value can be included in a measure of economic benefits. This means that some of the effects of regulation cannot be valued in economic terms. For example, ecological effects, such as alterations in species populations or subtle changes in ecological systems, may have no perceptible effect on individual welfare. If such effects are not arguments in individuals' utility functions, no willingness to pay or compensation measures can be derived. Thus there are no economic benefits or costs associated with such changes. Yet many people would argue that these effects are important and should be taken into account in environmental decisionmaking. The problem is that their importance, whatever it is, cannot be captured within the conventional economic rubric. This must be acknowledged as a limitation of the economic approach to environmental decisionmaking.

The third problem is the value judgment concerning equity, namely, that society is indifferent to the distribution of benefits and costs. It is a value judgment that some people are reluctant to accept. And I suspect that this indifference to distributional consequences of public policy choice helps to explain the distrust with which some people view benefit-cost analysis as a decision rule for environmental regulation.

To summarize, in order to use benefit-cost analysis as a decision rule for environmental regulations, we must be able to obtain objective measures of the money values of beneficial and adverse effects; we must agree that those effects of environmental regulation which fall outside of the economic rubric do not matter; and we must agree on the value judgment that aggregate net benefits are to be maximized regardless of the distribution of benefits and costs. The state of the art of economic measurement is such that the first requirement is not satisfied for important categories of benefits and costs, such as reduced risk of death and preservation or enhancement of ecological systems not directly exploited by humans. The second two requirements involve value judgments, but as I understand the public debate on environmental policy, it appears that there are many who would reject one or both of these value judgments.[5] For these reasons, I am reluctant to advocate requiring benefit-cost analysis as a decision rule for environmental regulations.

This is not the only way to view benefit-cost analysis. The decisionmaker wishing to weigh the positive and negative aspects of a proposed action needs a framework for organizing available information. Benefit-cost analysis, with its rules for defining and measuring beneficial and adverse effects, provides such a framework. The benefit-cost analyst can use the accepted procedures for organizing and presenting what is known about the benefits and costs of alternative actions. In those rare cases where the analyst can present a complete and accurate description of all of the consequences of the proposed action in economic terms, the decisionmaker will have been given valuable information. Nevertheless, because of concern for the distributional consequences of a proposal, the decisionmaker may choose not to act on the basis of a net benefit criterion.

More typically, there will be gaps in the information on values and consequences that lie outside of the benefit-cost rubric. In such cases, the analyst must present the decisionmaker with as much quantitative and descriptive information as possible. For the decisionmaker, subjective judgments and balancing unavoidably play a role in the actual decisions. The decisionmaker must introduce his own qualitative judgments about the relative weights or values to be placed on different, noncommensurable objectives. From this perspective, benefit-cost analysis can aid decisionmakers by systematically organizing and presenting the information on consequences and tradeoffs. But it should not dictate choices, nor should it replace the ultimate responsibility of politically accountable decisionmakers.[6]

In light of this discussion, I would like to comment briefly on the recently issued Executive Order 12291. Two provisions of this order are pertinent. Section 3 states in part:

> . . . each agency shall, in connection with every major rule, prepare, and to the extent permitted by law consider, a Regulatory Impact Analysis. . . .each . . . Regulatory Impact Analysis shall contain the following information:
>
> (1) A description of the potential benefits of the rule, including any beneficial effects that cannot be quantified in monetary terms, and the identification of those likely to receive the benefits;
>
> (2) A description of the potential costs of the rule, including any adverse effects that cannot be quantified in monetary terms, and the identification of those likely to bear the costs;

(3)   A determination of the potential net benefits of the rule, including an evaluation of the effects that cannot be quantified in monetary terms.

Section 2 of the order states:

. . . in promulgating new regulations, reviewing existing regulations, and developing legislative proposals concerning regulation, all agencies, to the extent permitted by law, shall adhere to the following requirements:
(b)   Regulatory action shall not be undertaken unless the potential benefits to society for the regulation outweigh the potential costs to society;
(c)   Regulatory objectives shall be chosen to maximize the net benefits to society.

I interpret Section 3 to be calling for the presentation of all relevant information to the decisionmaker employing the framework of benefit-cost analysis, but explicitly acknowledging that not all of the relevant consequences of regulatory actions can be captured and measured in monetary terms in a benefit-cost framework. It also reflects a recognition that decisionmakers may be concerned with the incidence of benefits and costs and calls for the presentation of distributional information to the decisionmaker. This section of the order is consistent with the view expressed here that benefit-cost analysis is a valuable framework for describing the consequences of a proposed regulation.

Section 2 of the order seems misguided in several respects. First, it appears to call for making decisions on the basis of aggregate net benefits, without regard for the distribution of benefits and costs. Thus, it would sanction policies that imposed uncompensated costs on some groups so long as aggregate benefits were greater than aggregate costs. This might be justified in those cases where gains and losses to individuals were small relative to their initial income, or where beneficiaries were forced to bear a substantial portion of the costs. But, for example, where changes in the risk of death are involved and where a regulatory decision increases the risk of death to one group of the population while conferring benefits in the form of higher incomes or lower prices on a different group, some people would argue that the uneven incidence of benefits and costs should be reflected in the final decision.[7]

Second, by calling for the maximization of net benefits, this section ignores the possibility that some beneficial effects may not be measurable in monetary terms. At least it gives no guidance to the decisionmaker as to how to proceed when net benefits cannot be calculated. The draft guidelines issued by the Office of Management and Budget on June 5, 1981 state that the monetary net benefit estimate should be accompanied by information on nonmonetary, but quantifiable effects and nonquantifiable effects "in a way that facilitates making an informed final decision." But in a section entitled "Rationale for Choosing the Proposed Regulatory Action," the guidelines state, "Ordinarily the regulatory alternative selected should be the one that achieves the greatest net benefits." Third, this section does not give any guidance to the decisionmaker as to what consequences, if any, other than economic benefits and costs, should be taken into account in making regulatory decisions. Thus, it increases the danger that decisionmakers will ignore those effects that cannot be expressed in monetary terms that are commensurate with economic benefits and costs. In sum, Section 2 of the order appears to place too great a burden on benefit-cost analysis and to focus the attention of decisionmakers on too narrow a range of potential consequences.

Incorporating Uncertainty

In the preceding discussion of benefit-cost analysis it was implicitly assumed that the values for relevant physical and economic variables were known with certainty. But this will almost never be perfectly true, and often there is substantial uncertainty regarding the values of key parameters in the analysis. There are three major sources of this uncertainty. First, although it is commonly believed that estimating the costs of controlling pollution is straightforward, it is often difficult to predict which of several technological options will be chosen by those affected by regulations. It is also difficult to predict the costs of relatively untried control technologies and the nature and extent of likely induced innovation in response to new control requirements. Second, there is typically uncertainty about the properties of the dose-effect relationship and the magnitude of the risks for substances that affect human health. These uncertainties stem from the difficulties in carrying out proper epidemiological studies on humans and from the problems in extrapolating from high-dose animal feeding studies to low-dose human exposures. Third, there may be uncertainty about the appropriate shadow prices to be used in converting known physical effects into monetary benefits or costs.

As is well known from decision theory, a logical approach to dealing with uncertainty is to assign probabilities to the alternative possible magnitudes of the relevant variables and to use the laws of probability to compute expected values, confidence intervals, and so forth.[8] For example, suppose a scientist says about a certain chemical, "My best judgment is that the chemical in the environment is harmless; but there is a small chance that it might be highly toxic to humans." The statement conveys the fact that there is uncertainty. But it does not convey any useful information about the nature and magnitude of the uncertainty. First, what does "highly toxic" mean? Second, how small is a "small chance"? Both statements are qualitative statements about potentially quantifiable magnitudes. As such, they can be interpreted in different ways by different people.

Probabilities provide a means of reducing the ambiguity of statements about uncertainty. Probability theory provides an unambiguous and logical way to reason about the implications of uncertainty. With some additional work, the above statements might be translated into the language of probability theory as follows:

> I estimate the probability to be 0.05 that the chemical will result in the rate of 100 deaths per 100,000 exposed population per year as a result of unrestricted use; the probability is 0.05 that the chemical will result in additional deaths at the rate of 10 deaths per 100,000 exposed population per year; and the probability is 0.9 that the chemical is harmless.

The basis of the probabilities in this statement is not objective in the sense of being derived from logical analysis of the processes involved or derived inferentially from observations of repeated trials. Rather, the probabilities represent subjective judgments that summarize information or a state of mind. The difficulty of encoding such judgments in the form of probabilities is not trivial. But it is logically equivalent to asking oneself to state the probability or odds at which he would be willing to bet on the occurrence of the uncertain event in question.[9]

Given uncertainty, the appropriate framework for organizing information is the probability framework. The analyst should report to the decisionmaker the possible alternative values for uncertain parameters and the probabilities attached to each. It will also be useful to the decisionmaker to have summary measures of this probability information, specifically the expected value of each uncertain parameter and some measure of the dispersion of possible values, for example, the standard deviation or a 95 percent confidence interval.

Suppose that the information on the consequences of a policy, including the summary measures reflecting uncertainty, is given to the decisionmaker. What guidance can be given to the decisionmaker as to how to use this information in choosing among regulatory options? If he has accepted the conditions that permit the use of benefit-cost analysis as a decision rule, and if he is risk neutral, then the decision rule should be to adopt policies with positive expected values of net benefits or to choose those options with the highest expected values of net benefits.

As is well known, risk neutrality is equivalent to having a constant marginal utility of income or, in this case, of net benefits. But a decisionmaker's attitude toward social welfare need not be consistent with constant marginal utility of income. For example, suppose a chemical is being considered for use. Suppose also that the probability is 0.9 that net benefits will be $1 million and that the probability is 0.1 that because of adverse health effects the net benefits will be −$8 million. The expected value of the net benefits of using the chemical is $1 million. A risk neutral decisionmaker would allow the chemical in use. But many decisionmakers might feel that because of the nontrivial possibility of a large negative benefit, the prudent thing to do would be to ban the chemical. If the chemical were banned, the decisionmaker would reveal risk aversion by his choice.[10]

Should regulatory decisionmakers be risk neutral or risk averse? In another context, that of determining the appropriate discount rate for benefit-cost analysis, appeal is often made to arguments of risk pooling and risk spreading to justify the choice of a risk-free discount rate. But at least for some types of environmental hazards these arguments may not justify risk neutrality in social decisionmaking. Risk pooling applies in those situations where as the number of trials (or, in this case, chemicals to be regulated) increases, the variance in the outcome decreases. Risk pooling requires that each regulation be, in effect, an independent trial. But, for example, if animal-to-human extrapolation models consistently underestimate or overestimate risks to human health, adverse outcomes are correlated, and the aggregation of risks does not reduce the variance in the outcomes. Risk spreading applies where a given net benefit or cost is spread over a large number of individuals so that the effect of the outcome on any one individual is insignificant. But for environmental health hazards, adverse outcomes include increases in the number of deaths. And these by their nature cannot be spread over the total population.

Risk aversion on the part of decisionmakers may be justified in some circumstances. But this is not to say that decisionmakers are or should be risk averse. If they are risk averse, then maximizing the expected net benefit cannot be invoked as a decision rule, and the analyst must present information on not only expected values, but also some measure of the variance in outcomes. The decisionmaker's choice will ultimately reflect some tradeoff between net benefits and the avoidance of some types of adverse outcomes.

Cost-Effectiveness Analysis

This decisionmaking framework involves the establishment of some target level of beneficial effect, for example, an ambient air quality standard, and the selection of a mix of policy options to achieve that target at a minimum cost. It can be used in circumstances where cost information on alternative regulatory options is available, but benefit information is not. The cost-effectiveness criterion ranks alternative policies in terms of the cost of achieving the given target. Since all policies being evaluated achieve the same target, they have the same level of beneficial effects. Thus, policy alternatives differ only in terms of their monetary costs. By structuring the range of alternatives to be evaluated, the problems created by the fact that benefits and costs are not both measured in monetary units can be avoided. Cost-effectiveness analysis can be useful in evaluating alternative instruments for achieving given goals. But it cannot be used to address the more fundamental question of what the goals or targets should be. The latter question requires, implicitly or explicitly, a weighing of benefits against costs.

Total costs of achieving a given target are minimized when each option is pushed to the point where the marginal costs of all options are equal. Cost-effectiveness analysis requires that information be obtained on the incremental or marginal costs of the alternatives being considered.

THE REGULATORY ANALYSIS FOR POLYCHLORINATED BIPHENYLS

The principal legal authority for EPA's regulation of polychlorinated biphenyls (PCBs) is Section 6(e) of the Toxic Substances Control Act

(PL 94-469). This section requires that EPA promulgate regulations covering the disposal of PCBs. It also bans the manufacture, processing, or use of PCBs in other than "a totally enclosed manner." Finally, the law authorizes EPA to make exceptions to the ban on other than totally enclosed uses if it finds that "such manufacture, processing, distribution in commerce, or use . . . will not present an *unreasonable risk* of injury to health or the environment" (emphasis added).[11]

EPA has issued two major sets of regulations under the authority of Section 6(e). The first set covered disposal and marking and was issued in February 1978 (EPA 1978a). The second set implemented the ban on manufacturing, processing, and use and provided exceptions as authorized by the law (EPA 1979c). The purpose of this section is to discuss the information provided in support of the regulations governing manufacturing, use, and so forth, and the relationship of these regulations to those governing marking and disposal and to other policy options affecting the risks posed by PCBs in the environment.

The proposed rules were published for comment in the *Federal Register* in June 1978 (EPA 1978b). The major provisions of the proposed regulations were to:

1. authorize continued use of transformers (other than in railroad cars) under certain conditions;
2. require incineration or disposal in chemical landfill for PCB contaminated mineral oil drained from transformers;
3. authorize use of PCB contaminated transformers in railroads for five years with a phased reduction in the concentration of PCBs in transformer fluids;
4. require the replacement of PCB contaminated motors in mining equipment;
5. require the replacement of PCB contaminated fluids in hydraulic die casting systems;
6. authorize the continued use of PCB contaminated carbonless copy paper; and
7. ban the use of electromagnets containing PCB fluids.

The discussion of the proposed rules included approximately one page of economic analysis describing the total costs of complying with each proposed ban or restriction on use and proposed disposal requirement. The *Federal Register* notice did not include any data on the quantities of PCBs affected by the various provisions. There were no data on the costs which would be incurred if some of the proposed authorized uses were banned. And there were no data on the probabilities that any of the not totally enclosed uses being considered might lead to releases to the environment or to human exposures. Thus, the economic data were not related in any meaningful way to the choices open to EPA.

The final regulations adopted in May 1979 were different in two major respects. First, the regulation governing the disposal of contaminated mineral oil was modified to allow the use of the oil as a fuel in certain high efficiency boilers. This was permitted on grounds of cost-effectiveness. And PCB-containing electromagnets were defined as a totally enclosed use since the probability of release to the environment was considered to be negligible.

The analysis accompanying the proposed and final rules was deficient in at least two major respects. First, it provided no basis for assessing the cost-effectiveness of alternative regulations in reducing the risks posed by PCBs in the environment. Second, the information provided no basis for assessing the "reasonableness" of the risks remaining after the implementation of the regulations, or to put it differently, the unreasonableness of those risks eliminated by the regulations.

During the period that the regulations were being considered by EPA, a committee of the National Academy of Sciences (NAS) was preparing an assessment of PCBs in the environment under a contract with the Office of Research and Development of EPA. The report was issued in early 1979, but was apparently too late to influence EPA's analysis of the proposed regulations.[12]

The NAS report assessed the cost-effectiveness of alternative policy options for reducing the risks of PCBs in the environment, and it included a health risk assessment and a tentative benefit-cost analysis. Uncertainties were reflected in the risk assessment, but not in the formal probability language described above.

Since PCBs are very stable in the environment and since they become widely dispersed, the prevention of releases of PCBs to the environment can be used as a measure of the effectiveness of alternative regulations. The NAS committee used data provided by EPA and by its economic contractor to estimate the cost-effectiveness of the then-existing and proposed EPA regulations. Cost-effectiveness was measured by the cost per kilogram (kg) of PCBs controlled by each specified regulation. The cost-effectiveness measures are summarized in Table 4-1. Because of limitations in the available data, not all of the proposed regulations are included in this table. The table shows that as measured by the average cost per kg controlled, the cost effectiveness of the alternatives analyzed varies by a factor of 200,000. The options listed would, if implemented, control a total of 260 million kg of PCBs. Virtually all of this control is accomplished with options A through E at average costs of $33 per kg or less. The remaining options listed (F through I) would contribute less than 0.1 percent to further controls of PCBs, while virtually doubling the total cost of regulation. On the assumption that within each option there is no variation in the cost per kg controlled under different circumstances, the incremental costs of Table 4-1 can be interpreted as marginal costs of control.[13] The data then imply a very steeply rising marginal cost of control for PCBs.

Cost minimization requires that all lower cost options be exhausted before a higher cost option is considered. In its final rulemaking, EPA adopted all of the proposed regulations in Table 4-1 except option F, replacement of PCB-containing electromagnets. Thus it would appear that the cost-effectiveness of PCB regulation could be improved by relaxing one of the higher cost options and banning PCB-containing electromagnets. But this points out one of the limitations in the data presented by the NAS committee. Specifically, the cost-effectiveness measure is based on the implicit assumption that for each of the options the probability is 1.0 that the PCBs would reach the environment if the regulation were not adopted. The cost-effectiveness measure should be an expected value based on the probability that the control option would reduce the flow of PCBs to the environment. Since EPA decided not to regulate PCB-containing electromagnets, they were implicitly making this kind of calculation. But it would be better if the calculations and the underlying assumptions about probabilities were made explicit. The cost-effectiveness of a ban on the use of existing stocks of carbonless copy paper was not analyzed. Thus, there is no analytical basis for evaluating the EPA decision not to ban this nonenclosed use.

The steeply rising marginal cost curve for control shows the importance of considering where to draw the line, that is, how to balance the increase in control costs against the benefits of reduced risks of damage due to PCBs in the environment. The law requires EPA to protect against "unreasonable risk." There has been considerable

Table 4-1.   Costs and Quantities Controlled for EPA Regulations on Use and Disposal.

Policy	Quantity Controlled (kg)	Control Costs[a] ($)	Average Cost Per kg ($)
A. Incinerate fluids from PCB transformers (required)	123,000,000	75,000,000	0.61
B. Shred and incinerate high voltage capacitors (required)	90,900,000	350,000,000	3.85
C. Shred and incinerate low voltage capacitors (required)	31,800,000	143,000,000	4.49
D. Flush and drain transformers after A. (required)	12,300,000	105,000,000	8.50
E. Place transformers in chemical waster landfill (required)[b]	1,360,000	45,100,000	33.16
F. Replace PCB-containing electro-magnets and incinerate fluid (proposed)	100,000–150,000	2,800,000–3,400,000	18.67–34.00
G. Replace PCB-containing motors in mining equipment (proposed)			
(1) Loaders	13,000	2,000,000	155.00
(2) Continuous Miners	1,136	640,000–2,240,000	563.00–1,972.00
H. Drain and incinerate mineral oil transformer fluids if contaminated by more than 50 ppm PCBs (proposed)[c,d]	10,900	612,000,000–769,000,000	70,000.00–88,000.00

Table 4–1 (continued)

Policy	Quantity Controlled (kg)	Control Costs[a]	Average Cost Per kg ($)
I. Flush and replace contaminated hydraulic fluids in die casting (proposed)	data incomplete[e]	data incomplete[e]	133,000.00

[a]Options A through E will be undertaken as PCB-containing equipment is taken out of service. For example some PCB-containing transformers may remain in service for up to forty years. The control costs here will be incurred over the useful life of the equipment in question. These costs have not been discounted to the present. Discounting would reduce computed control costs, and would have the greatest effect on control options affecting transformers and transformer fluids. Discounting would have relatively little effect on options F through I, since these options would have to be undertaken shortly after the effective date of the proposed regulations.

[b]It is assumed that transformers will be disposed of in chemical waste landfills rather than by incineration.

[c]Fluids with greater than 500 ppm are covered by Policy A.

[d]The final regulations permitted burning fluids in high-efficiency boilers at substantially lower costs per kg. Costs were estimated at $1,000–5,000 per kg. See Environmental Protection Agency (1979a:44–71).

[e]Incremental costs are estimated from average costs per die-casting machine. Aggregate costs and quantity controlled are not known because of lack of data on the number of affected machines.

Source: National Academy of Sciences (1979:86–87).

debate about the meaning of the term unreasonable risk and how to determine the reasonableness of a given risk. There is one interpretation of the term that is consistent with the economic choice-theoretic principles underlying the benefit-cost analysis framework. This interpretation states that a risk is unreasonable if the aggregate willingness to pay to avoid that risk is greater than the cost of avoiding it.

Based on this interpretation, the NAS Committee undertook a risk-benefit assessment of the regulatory alternatives. The only risk considered was the risk to human health due to cancer induced by PCB intake. To the extent that effects on human health other than cancer occur at present doses, or that effects on nonhuman species matter, the benefits of PCB control will be understated. Based on a range of values of avoiding cancer deaths of $100 thousand to $1 million per death avoided, the committee estimated the benefits of controlling PCBs released to the environment to be between $30 and 300 per kg.[14] If the two alternative values for cancer death avoidance are deemed equally likely, the expected value of benefits is $165 per kg. An expected value maximizer would choose options A through G (1), but would decline to undertake options G (2) through I. The NAS Committee stated that its assessment of cancer risk could be overstated or understated by a factor of 100. Thus, there is a high variance in the estimate of benefits per kg. A risk averse decisionmaker would wish to take this into account in deciding where to draw the line.[15]

Even if the decisionmaker is unwilling to specify a value of life for use by the analyst in calculating the net benefits of regulatory alternatives, the risk and cost data can still be useful in illuminating the nature of the tradeoffs and the value implications of alternative choices. For example, given the cancer risk assessment underlying the benefit-cost calculation, the minimum value of life necessary to justify each regulatory alternative can be calculated. The committee estimated that 8 kg of PCBs distributed in the diet of the U.S. population would result in one additional cancer death. It also estimated that one of every 400 kg of PCBs released to the environment would eventually find its way into the human diet. Thus there would be 1/3200 cancer cases per kg of PCBs released.

Option F has a cost of $34.00 kg controlled. Given the assumptions this translates to a cost of $109,000 per cancer case avoided. Unless the decisionmaker were willing to have society incur at least this much per death avoided, Option F should not be undertaken. These data can also be used to estimate the value of deaths avoided which is implied by any regulatory decision. Option G would cost $6.3 mil-

lion per death avoided. If the decisionmaker chose Option F but declined to undertake Option G, his implicit value of life would be
greater than $109,000 but less than $6.3 million.

So far, the discussion has been limited to EPA's regulatory options
under Section 6 (e) of the Toxic Substances Control Act. In principle,
there are three ways to reduce the PCB risks to humans:

- reduce the flow of additional PCBs to the environment;
- control the exposure of people to PCBs already in the environment; and
- reduce the stocks of PCBs already in the environment.

At the same time that EPA was considering ways to reduce releases
of PCBs to the environment, the Food and Drug Administration was
considering maximum allowable concentrations of PCBs in foods, including fish. And several proposals were being considered for dredging and safely disposing of contaminated sediments from the Hudson
River. The NAS committee computed cost-effectiveness measures
for these options on a comparable basis, that is, on a cost per kg controlled equivalent.[16] These estimates are presented in Table 4–2.

Table 4-2. The Cost-Effectiveness of Limiting Fish Contamination and of Dredging Contaminated Sediments.

Option	Incremental Quantity Controlled (kg)	Average Cost Per kg ($)
Dredging remnant deposits (completed)	7,700	219
Hot spot dredging (recommended— approval pending)	77,000	291
Maximum of 2 ppm of PCBs in fish (adopted)	25,600	312
Maximum of 1 ppm of PCBs in fish (rejected)	13,600	731
Remove all river sediments (not presently under consideration)	55,600	9,450

Source: National Academy of Sciences (1979: Chapter 2).

A comparison with Table 4-1 shows that the government has not been consistent in its decisions regarding the reduction of risk due to PCBs. It has declined to incur costs of $731 per kg to reduce risk through the control of PCBs in the diet, while it has incurred costs of over 100 times that amount to prevent the risks associated with releases from contaminated hydraulic fluids. As the NAS committee concluded:

> Economic analyses should include cost data on all options—not just those under a single agency's regulatory authority. The analysis could then show—as does the analysis presented in this report—that some options beyond a particular agency's authority may be substantially more cost-effective than some that lie within the agency's jurisdiction. A comprehensive, coordinated government policy toward control of pollutants should reflect such findings.[17]

To summarize this discussion of the regulatory analysis of PCBs, the data presented to EPA did not include statements of the cost-effectiveness of options accepted and of those available but not proposed (for example, a ban on carbonless copy paper), or of options being considered or already decided upon by other agencies. Thus, EPA had no basis for selecting a cost-minimizing mix of regulatory options. Yet cost-effectiveness measures could be calculated from available data and presented in a framework which made more clear the tradeoffs among policy options. Furthermore, the data presented to EPA did not include any estimates of the reductions in risk due to PCBs in the environment. EPA had no systematic basis for making determinations of unreasonable risk according to Section 6 (e). It is true that estimates of both control costs and reductions in risk cannot be made with certainty, and in some cases the ranges of uncertainty may be quite wide. But as long as the nature of this uncertainty is made clear to the decisionmaker, the additional information should lead to better informed decisions.

CONCLUDING OBSERVATIONS

Decisionmakers should have information on the risks, benefits, and costs of alternative regulatory options. Since there is likely to be uncertainty in the estimates of one or more of the relevant variables, the information should be presented using the consistent language of probability, that is, in terms of expected values and some measure of dispersion. The principles of benefit-cost analysis provide a basis for defining and measuring benefits and costs. These principles also indicate that the data should be used to determine incremental benefits and costs, to identify tradeoffs at the margin, and to identify opportunities to increase the cost-effectiveness of any regulatory effort.

Advocating the presentation of information in a benefit-cost framework is not advocating that regulatory decisions be made according to a benefit-cost rule. The state of the art often does not permit the determination of the required values or shadow prices in a manner satisfactory to all of the affected parties. Furthermore, the use of benefit-cost analysis to make decisions requires the acceptance of controversial value judgments: that only those things that can be captured in the rubric of benefit-cost analysis and applied welfare theory should matter; and that we should be indifferent to the distribution of the benefits and costs of regulatory policy. Finally, decisionmakers may be risk averse.

If the benefit-cost rule is not accepted, decisionmakers are left with the responsibility for making their own balancing judgments. They should be provided with the best possible information on the opportunity set they face so that they can see more clearly the value implications of the particular choices they may be inclined to make. There is a temptation to give advice as to how this balancing should be done, for example, how much weight to give to nonmonetized or nonquantifiable effects, such as impacts on regional employment and income. But there is no objective or scientific basis for giving advice of this sort. For example, the logic of benefit-cost analysis leads to the conclusion that purely pecuniary effects and redistributions, such as those associated with localized employment impacts, can be ignored. But this conclusion follows from a specific value judgment about the role of distributional considerations in regulatory decisionmaking. The continuing concern of political decisionmakers about regional employment suggests that, for better or worse, they do not share that value judgment.

The fact that benefit-cost analysis as a decision rule requires that a decisionmaker ignore a class of effects he knows to be important may help to explain the reluctance of decisionmakers to make greater use of benefit-cost analysis as an analytical tool. The relationship between the analyst and the decisionmaker might be improved if the latter could be induced to be more explicit about his value judgments. Then the analyst could gather and organize the data relevant to the decisionmaker's values.

A good analysis should show the implications of pushing certain assumptions about key variables, such as dose-response functions and shadow prices, through to their logical conclusions. In this way, the analysis can give the decisionmaker a better idea of the properties of the opportunity set while leaving the necessary tradeoffs to his discretion.

Benefit-cost analysis has been described here as a partial equilibrium and piecemeal form of analysis. It examines the consequences of one policy option at a time under the assumption that all other things are held constant. There may be types of problems for which the partial equilibrium, piecemeal approach could yield misleading results. For example, suppose that the net benefits of Regulation A depend on whether or not Regulation B is adopted, and that the net benefits of B depend, in turn, on the decision concerning A.[18] The evaluation of regulations in such cases requires a more comprehensive analytical framework, one that can evaluate mixes of alternatives. Linear or nonlinear programming techniques may be useful. However, in order to fit these problems into a programming framework it may be necessary to ignore important consequences.

In a section entitled "Never Believe A Competent Benefit-Cost Analysis," Lave (1972) argues that good analyses are likely to overstate costs and understate benefits. I would go one step further and say that a competently done benefit-cost analysis should clarify why it should not be believed, or at least not be taken literally. The presentation of the analysis should include a discussion of the weaknesses and limitations of the data and the critical assumptions used to reach the conclusions. It should state what simplifying assumptions have been made in order to make the analytical problems tractable. The discussion should make the uncertainties in parameter estimates and values explicit. It should include a qualitative discussion of those consequences of the proposed regulation that do not lend themselves to quantitative economic analysis, or that lie outside the rubric of conventional economics but may nevertheless be important to decisionmakers.

Unfortunately, this advice to be frank about the limitations of analysis is not likely to be helpful to decisionmakers operating in the adversarial setting of the U.S. legal and regulatory institutions where decisions are likely to be challenged in court and subjected to judicial review. To the extent that judicial review is substantive rather than simply procedural, the strengths and limitations of the analysis underlying the decision will become an issue. As a consequence, the agency will be tempted to tailor its analysis to be a justification of a particular alternative—the one chosen—rather than an objective examination of the consequences of alternatives. It is difficult to conceive of a solution to this problem within the context of existing political and legal institutions.

NOTES

1. Analytical frameworks for regulatory decisionmaking for environmental problems are also discussed in National Academy of Sciences (1975) (especially in Appendix H), and in National Academy of Sciences (1977a, 1977b). For further discussion of the principles of benefit-cost analysis and their relationship to the underlying principles of welfare evaluation, see Prest and Turvey (1965), and Haveman and Weisbrod (1975).

2. For discussion of techniques for estimating the benefits of environmental improvement, see Freeman (1979).

3. Or more generally, the rule is to choose that option with the highest net benefits, that is, the one for which marginal benefits just equal marginal costs.

4. Uncertainty about underlying technical relationships is not a barrier to the application of benefit-cost analysis. As discussed in the next section, uncertainties can be expressed and described in terms of probabilities and benefit-cost analysis carried forward using expected values.

5. For criticisms of the use of benefit-cost analysis for regulatory decisionmaking on these and other grounds, see, for example, Baram (1980), Ashford (1981), and Bradford and Feiveson (1976).

6. This is the point of view adopted in National Academy of Sciences (1975).

7. For example, see Baram (1980) and Ashford (1981).

8. For a discussion of probability theory in the context of environmental decisionmaking, see National Academy of Sciences (1975). A basic reference on decision theory is Raiffa (1968).

9. For further discussion of risk assessment procedures and the estimation of probabilities, see Chapter 3.

10. It should be noted that risk aversion does not always bias decisions toward environmental protection. For a chemical already in use, the expected value of regulation must be sufficiently large to compensate for the risk that the chemical is in fact not dangerous to health and control costs will have been incurred unnecessarily. In this case, risk

aversion biases decisions toward no regulation, in comparison with risk-neutral decisionmaking. This is true whether the uncertainty is in the measure of the benefits of control or the costs of control, since either type of uncertainty increases the variance of net benefits.

11. The Environmental Protection Agency has also issued effluent limitation regulations under the authority of the Federal Water Pollution Control Act Amendments of 1972. These regulations are not the concern of this section.

12. See Environmental Protection Agency (1979b:106), and the report in National Academy of Sciences (1979). I was a member of the committee that prepared the report.

13. This is an example of a simplifying assumption employed to make the analysis tractable.

14. For the details of this calculation, see National Academy of Sciences (1979:93–96, 137–42).

15. Since the regulatory options involve controls on existing uses of PCBs, the risk-averse decisionmaker would require benefits of control in excess of costs in order to justify undertaking the risk that regulations might impose costs greater than benefits. Thus, as argued above, the risk-averse decisionmaker would regulate less strictly. The decisionmaker who would adopt more strict regulation, for example, option G(2), reveals either of two things: he holds a higher subjective value of avoiding cancer deaths or a higher subjective assessment of cancer risk due to PCBs than those used in this analysis; or he has adopted a lexicographic social preference ordering that places reduction in health risk above other social goods.

16. See National Academy of Sciences (1979:85–93).

17. See National Academy of Sciences (1979:99–100).

18. In Chapter 2, Dorfman suggests that pesticide regulation problems often have this property.

REFERENCES

Ashford, Nicholas. 1981. "Alternatives to Cost-Benefit Analysis in Regulatory Decisions." *Annals of the New York Academy of Sciences* 363: 129–37.

Baram, Michael S. 1980. "Cost-Benefit Analysis; An Inadequate Basis for Health, Safety, and Environmental Regulatory Decisionmaking." *Ecology Law Quarterly* 8, no. 3:473–531.

Bradford, David, and Harold A. Feiveson, 1976. "Benefits and Costs, Winners and Losers." In *Boundaries of Analysis: An Inquiry into the*

Tocks Island Dam Controversy, edited by Harold A. Feiveson, Frank W. Sinden, and Robert H. Socolow. Cambridge, Mass.: Ballinger Publishing Company.

Environmental Protection Agency. 1978a. "Polychlorinated Biphenyls (PCBs): Disposal and Marking." *Federal Register* 43, no. 34 (February 17):7150–64.

Environmental Protection Agency. 1978b. "Polychlorinated Biphenyls (PCBs): Manufacturing, Processing, Distribution in Commerce, and Use Bans." *Federal Register* 43, no. 110 (June 7):24802–17.

Environmental Protection Agency. 1979a. *PCB Manufacturing, Processing, Distribution in Commerce, and Use Ban Regulation: Economic Impact Analysis.* (March). Washington, D.C.

Environmental Protection Agency. 1979b. *Support Documents/Voluntary Environmental Impact Statement.* (April). Washington, D.C.

Environmental Protection Agency. 1979c. "Polychlorinated Biphenyls (PCBs): Manufacturing, Processing, Distribution in Commerce, and Use Bans." *Federal Register* 44, no. 106 (May 31):31514–68.

Freeman, A. Myrick III. 1979. *The Benefits of Environmental Improvement: Theory and Practice.* Baltimore: Johns Hopkins Press.

Haveman, Robert H., and Burton A. Weisbrod. 1975. "The Concept of Benefits and Cost-Benefit Analysis: With Emphasis on Water Pollution Control Activities." In *Cost-Benefit Analysis and Water Pollution Policy,* edited by Henry M. Peskin and Eugene P. Seskin, pp. 37–66. Washington, D.C.: Urban Institute.

Lave, Lester B. 1972. "Air Pollution Damage: Some Difficulties in Estimating the Value of Abatement." In *Environmental Quality Analysis: Theory and Methodology in the Social Sciences,* edited by Allen V. Kneese and Blair T. Bower, pp. 238–39. Baltimore: Johns Hopkins Press.

National Academy of Sciences. 1975. *Decision Making for Regulating Chemicals in the Environment.* Washington, D.C.

National Academy of Sciences. 1977a. *Decision Making in the Environmental Protection Agency.* Washington, D.C.

National Academy of Sciences. 1977b. *Decision Making in the Environmental Protection Agency—Selected Working Papers.* Washington, D.C.

National Academy of Sciences. 1979. *Polychlorinated Biphenyls.* Washington, D.C.

Prest, A.R., and Ralph Turvey. 1965. "Cost-Benefit Analysis: A Survey." *Economic Journal* 75, no. 4 (December):683–735.

Raiffa, Howard. 1968. *Decision Analysis: Introductory Lectures on Choices under Uncertainty.* Reading, Mass.: Addison-Wesley.

Reagan, Ronald. 1981. "Executive Order No. 12291." *Federal Register* 46, no. 33 (February 19):13193–98.

5 TRUTH AND CONSEQUENCES: SOME ROLES FOR SCIENTISTS AND ANALYSTS IN ENVIRONMENTAL DECISIONMAKING

James W. Vaupel

Environmental standards are brewed in a cauldron bubbling with physicians' diagnoses, toxicologists' findings, statisticians' formulas, economists' theories, lawyers' cautions, lobbyists' pressures, congressmen's questions, bureaucrats' wafflings, and judges' rulings. The purpose of this chapter is to provide some insights into how to improve the quality of this stew by thinking through, from a policy analyst's perspective, the nature of the contributions of scientists and analysts.

THREE IMAGES

Natural scientists, economists, and political scientists perceive the process of environmental standard-setting in radically different ways.[1]

This paper is based in part on my work as study director of the Committee on Risk and Decisionmaking of the National Academy of Sciences. I owe a particularly large intellectual debt to Howard Raiffa, who was chairman of that committee, and to John D. Graham, who was staff associate. In addition, I am heavily indebted to three EPA analysts, Thomas B. Feagans, Harvey M. Richmond, and Thomas McCurdy, who taught me not only much of what I know about the EPA, but also much of what I understand about the appropriate roles of scientists and analysts in environmental decisionmaking. I also thank Wesley A. Magat, Philip J. Cook, and Robert D. Behn for their invaluable suggestions.

The Perspective of Natural Scientists

Most natural scientists—and probably most laymen as well—have an image of the standard-setting process that might be caricatured as shown in Figure 5-1. According to this view, natural scientists do the crucial work of determining the health and environmental effects of a hazardous substance. Once these facts are determined, the administrator of the Environmental Protection Agency (EPA) has little discretion in making the more or less obvious decision about what level of the hazardous substance can be allowed if public health and the environment are to be protected.

This image underlies most health, safety, and environmental legislation. The Clean Air Act, for example, prescribes "ambient air quality standards the attainment and maintenance of which . . . are requisite to protect the public health."[2] The act similarly instructs the administrator to set national emission standards for hazardous air pollutants "at the level which in his judgment provides an ample margin of safety to protect the public health."[3] Both the Resource

Figure 5-1. Environmental Standard-Setting from the Perspective of Natural Scientists.

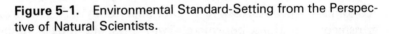

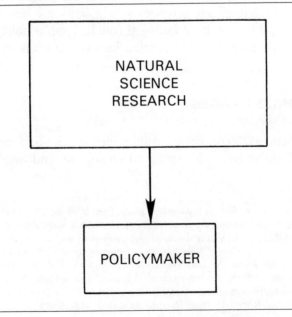

Conservation and Recovery Act and the Solid Waste Disposal Act require standards "as may be necessary to protect human health and the environment."[4] In addition to such "risk only" statutes, a number of "technology based" statutes are similar in spirit.[5] They protect public health and the environment as much as possible by requiring the "best practicable control technology." Examples include the Federal Water Pollution Control Act and the sections of the Clean Air Act dealing with new stationary sources of pollution.[6]

Furthermore, the natural scientists' image as depicted in Figure 5-1 roughly conforms to the actual division of labor in EPA: for any particular standard-setting decision, most of the available budget and most of the hours of effort are devoted to producing and assembling natural science facts.

The Perspective of Economists

Economists belittle the natural scientists' conception since it fails to consider costs. The economists' image is caricatured in Figure 5-2. In this view, natural scientists, with the help of some economists who do epidemiological research, do part of the work. Essentially, they estimate

Figure 5-2. Environmental Standard-Setting from the Perspective of Economists.

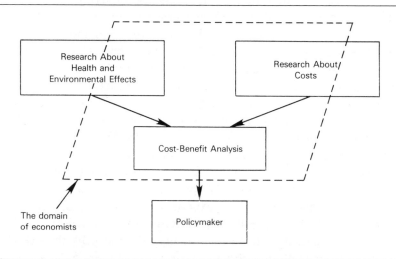

an exposure-response curve that describes the health and environmental effects of any particular level of exposure to a hazardous substance. Economists, perhaps with the help of some engineers, estimate how much it would cost to achieve any particular level of exposure. They then put the costs and benefits together in an analysis that informs the decisionmaker about the incremental costs of achieving the incremental benefits of stricter standards. Since it is not clear how much we as a society are willing to pay for health, safety, and environmental protection, the decisionmaker has some discretion. Most economists, however, think that in most cases they would be able to agree on a reasonable standard. Hence, the discretion in setting standards is not perceived as large.

The Perspective of Political Scientists

Political scientists—as well as most politicians—dismiss the images of both the natural scientists and the economists as naive and undemocratic. Like other major social decisions, environmental standards are set by a complex, interactive process involving numerous players contending in the political arena. The EPA administrator has severely circumscribed decisionmaking powers since he has to perform a complex balancing act to avoid antagonizing other power-holders, both within the agency and outside of it. Consider some of them. Congress determines budgets and can change statutes. Congress as a whole, the relevant oversight committees, and the key members and staff of these committees represent various levels of congressional authority. The White House, represented by the domestic policy staff of the president and by the Office of Management and Budget (OMB), can wield great power when the president decides to exercise it. Various business, labor, environmental, and consumer interest groups gain leverage through their influence on Congress and the White House, exerted through the press, lobbying, and campaign support.

Most political scientists agree that the process not only *does* but *should* work this way in a liberal, pluralistic democracy. Natural scientists, economists, and other experts are seen as actors in the ongoing political process, partially affecting environmental standards with their judgments, but in turn, being influenced by the other actors and by the changing climate of opinions. Figure 5-3 caricatures

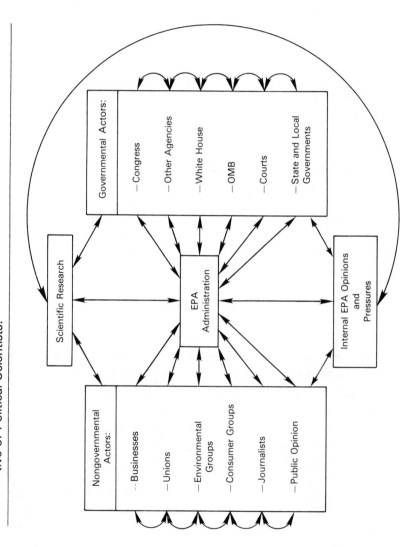

Figure 5-3. Environmental Standard-Setting from the Perspective of Political Scientists.

this image. An assiduous political scientist would include many more boxes and arrows and would attempt to convey the continuing flow of the evolving process.

Natural scientists, economists, and other experts often slip unintentionally into an undemocratic arrogance. If reminded, however, of the severe shortcomings of their knowledge and methods, and of the many advantages of a liberal society, at least the more realistic and judicious experts would have to agree that it would be a mistake to place environmental decisionmaking in the hands of a scientific elite that is insulated from politics. Even if experts could determine all the necessary facts about health, environmental, and economic effects with precision and consensus, and even if experts could be trusted to be honest, unbiased and disinterested, social value judgments would still have to be made in setting environmental standards. Different standards will benefit some people more than others and will be more consistent with some ethical beliefs and ideological perspectives than with others. In a democracy, such conflicts among competing interests and objectives are resolved by political processes in which many individuals have a voice.

A FOURTH IMAGE, FROM THE PERSPECTIVE OF POLICY ANALYSIS

A follower of the small and relatively new discipline known as policy analysis would not begrudge natural scientists credit for their key role in environmental standard-setting. A policy analyst would also sympathize with the economists' concern about costs and tradeoffs. And a policy analyst would agree with political scientists that most environmental decisions are and should be produced by the interaction of a large number of actors who jointly determine the trajectory of a policy.

The policy analyst, however, would view this interactive process not descriptively, but prescriptively from the following perspective. Consider one of the actors in the process—not necessarily the administrator of EPA, but perhaps a deputy assistant administrator, or perhaps a congressman, an official in OMB, the leader of an environmental organization, or the vice president for governmental relations of a large corporation. Consider this actor at some specific time when he has some discretion and thus must make a choice about what to do. The choice need not concern which environmental standard to recommend. It could concern any of the other decisions that must be made about how to influence, constrain, persuade, and educate others; about how to enforce decisions; about what kinds of authority to delegate and to whom; about what new information to gather, if any, about how to monitor and evaluate current policies; about how to defend policy decisions before courts, legislatures, superiors, outside interests, and the public; and so on. The policy-analysis question is: What kinds of information and analytical assistance might this decisionmaker find useful in helping him think about his particular decision problem?

A Suggestive Anecdote

That the policy-analysis perspective is far from obvious or trite was brought home to me at a doctoral examination. I was asked to help question a student who was studying environmental policymaking in a graduate department of environmental studies. The student, whom I had not met beforehand, had several years practical experience as a former employee of EPA. I asked him the following question: The administrator of EPA soon has to make a decision concerning which national ambient air quality standard to recommend for ozone. He has asked you to prepare a memo to help him make this decision. How would you organize the memo and what would you include in it.?

The student had three days to prepare an answer to this question as well as some other questions posed by other examiners. He came back with an outline of his memo to the EPA administrator. This outline, which ran for ten pages, was largely devoted to an impressively detailed breakdown of the results of various scientific studies of the health effects of ozone and had a brief final section summarizing the results of studies of "methods of control and costs."

Later, I asked an economics student, who had some familiarity with environmental issues, the same question. Her reply was that she would do a cost-benefit analysis. She would first estimate the costs of a broad range of standards, then she would estimate the monetary value of the health and environmental benefits of this range of standards. Finally, she would calculate the standard such that the estimated marginal costs just equalled the estimated marginal benefits.

Still later, I posed the same question in a policy-analysis seminar to a group of students who had done some reading about the ozone issue. The gist of their proposed memo ran roughly as follows:

> Currently the national ambient air quality standard for ozone is 0.08 parts per million. Business is pushing for a relaxation to 0.16 ppm while environmental groups want to maintain or even tighten the current standard. As discussed in section A, the available scientific and economic evidence, the weight of precedent, the balance of political pressures, and the protection of the agency's political base and internal morale constrain you to three possible recommendations—0.08, 0.10, or 0.12 ppm. The nature, distribution, and uncertainty surrounding various health and environmental benefits, economic costs, and political benefits and costs of 0.10 versus 0.08 and of 0.12 versus 0.10 are described in sections B and C. If you propose 0.08, you will probably be forced to retreat to 0.10 or even 0.12. Strategic considerations of this sort are discussed in section D.

The Fundamental Differences Between Scientific Research and Policy Analysis

This example is idiosyncratic and, like Figures 5–1, 5–2, and 5–3, a caricature. Nonetheless, I believe it is suggestive. Many natural scientists have a tendency to view policy problems in terms of a listing of facts rather than a listing of decision alternatives and the consequences of those alternatives. Many economists are willing to march relentlessly to a single cost-benefit comparison rather than present an array of kinds of advantages and disadvantages. And many scientists and economists confuse the general question of what is the socially optimal policy concerning ozone with the very specific question of what kinds of information a particular decisionmaker, with particular responsibilities and interests, at a particular moment in history, and in a particular political context, might want to have to help him think about his particular decision problem.

Most policy analyses are at least as qualitative as quantitative. The analyses suggest a framework of thought, they structure the decision alternatives, they describe the most important impacts of the alternatives, and they provide some guidance as to the most important trade-offs to be made. Sometimes the impacts and uncertainties surrounding the impacts are summarized numerically. Other times, crude qualitative rankings suffice (e.g., do asthmatics fare better, about the same, or worse with policy A versus B). Partial simplification of the array of costs and benefits may be made by collapsing sets of similar costs and benefits—not necessarily collapsing twenty different cost figures and twenty benefit figures down to one cost and one benefit figure, but, say, collapsing twenty cost figures into four cost indices and twenty benefit figures into six benefit indices. By simplifying a morass of data into a manageable set of summary indices, the decisionmaker may be in a better position to concentrate his attention on the crucial tradeoffs among a few incommensurable indices. The choice is not between no collapsing of costs and benefits and a mindless drive to a single number.

Scientists—and this includes not only natural scientists but also economists and other social and behavioral scientists—seek to discover the truth; policy analysts seek to improve the consequences of particular decisions. Scientists worry about statistical significance; policy analysts worry about social significance. Scientists are descriptive; policy analysts are prescriptive. The agenda for scientific research is set by the location of the points on the frontier of knowledge where breakthroughs are believed likely; the agenda for a policy analyst is set by the dilemmas faced at the moment by a specific decisionmaking client. Scientists rarely have to confront tradeoffs among conflicting objectives; policy analysts are continually confronted by such tradeoffs. Science aims for objective results; policy analysis is fundamentally subjective and deeply embedded in politics. Scientists strive for generalization, parsimony of theory, and elegance of formula; policy analysts focus on the specific details of unique problems. Scientists persevere in their research until the results are publishable; policy analysts attempt to do the best they can in the all-too-short time available. Scientists rejoice in research projects of breathtaking scope and grandeur—a theory of gravity, say, that governs atoms as well as galaxies or a theory of market transactions that explains the price of wine in 1920 in Canada as well as the price of wheat in 1990 in Portugal; policy analysts, to conserve their meager analytical resources, frugally tailor their highly selective and incomplete studies to focus on those few elements of a specific dilemma about which the decisionmaker is uncertain or perplexed.

Policy analysts are second-cousins to engineers, product designers, and architects. They are related to physicians who care for patients but have little in common with biomedical researchers. Policy analysis is a craft and an art, albeit an analytical craft and an art informed by research.

Economists and other social scientists often enter into political debates and think of themselves as policy analysts. But economists and other social scientists are also scientists. This dual role is the cause of much confusion. As penetratingly described in the essay, "Social Science and Policy Analysis: Some Fundamental Differences" (Moore 1980):

> In the typical social science publication, elaborate efforts are made to establish some relationship among some variables—say drug abuse and crime. The discussion of the data and methods of investigation is careful and restrained. The current investigation is placed in the context of other theories and findings. All this is consistent with the desire to build firm structures of knowledge slowly and carefully. Once the author has painstakingly established the existence (or non-existence) of a relationship, however, he turns to the "policy implications" of his finding. At this moment all the caution that characterized his analysis often leaves him, and he rushes toward conditionally prescriptive propositions at a pace that would make a serious policy analyst blush. Suddenly, goals are being suggested and governmental action conditionally prescribed all on the basis of *one* more or less firmly established empirical finding.

The author of this essay concludes that social scientists, if they were more aware of the nature of policy analysis, could be more constructive policy analysts. A more pessimistic conclusion seems at least equally justified: The differences in methods, perspectives, and concern for truth versus consequences between social science research and policy analysis are so profound that only rare ambidextrous geniuses will excel at both. Policy analysis may come more naturally to students educated in law or business (or, of course, policy analysis) than to students schooled in the methodology of (social or natural) scientific research.

A DECOMPOSITION OF ROLES

The dichotomy between policy analysis and scientific research by no means implies that natural and social scientists do not have crucially important roles to play in the process of environmental standard-setting. Policy analysts pick up the research findings and make do. If they had better information, they could do better.

When asked to suggest useful research topics to inform environmental decisionmaking,[7] natural scientists and social scientists tend to think about the hottest topics in their own disciplines. They usually fail to consider research needs in terms of the information a policymaker might want, and they also tend to be far too narrow in the range of topics they suggest. In setting an environmental standard, a policymaker might be interested in a broad range of human health effects, including:

1. How many people are or will be affected:
   a. in the entire population?
   b. in sensitive groups?
2. How much are they affected by:
   a. mortality?
   b. morbidity?
   c. severe pain and suffering?
   d. discomfort?
   e. anxiety?
3. Have they been classified by:
   a. age distribution?
   b. income distribution?
   c. race/ethnic background/sex?
   d. occupation?
   e. geographical location?
   f. quality of life/health status?
4. Will they be affected:
   a. now?
   b. with some time lag?
   c. in future generations?

In addition, the decisionmaker might be interested in various impacts on plant and animal life and on the aesthetic quality of the environment.

Similarly, a policymaker might value input from social science research about a wide range of policy effects, such as:

- Economic cost (and to whom),
- Effects on economic growth, productivity, and innovation,
- Effects on business competition,
- Economic and political effects on other countries,
- Effects on the distribution of income,
- Effects on public satisfaction with government,
- Legitimacy/fairness/symbolic importance as perceived by the public,
- Level and nature of political support and opposition,

- Effects on the quality of business and personal decisionmaking,
- Ease or difficulty of justification
  a. in court,
  b. in Congress,
  c. to the president,
  d. to the public,
- Enforcement costs, including costs of disrespect for the law engendered by unpunished violations.

Because many natural scientists fail to appreciate the nature and value of social science, and because many social scientists confuse their role as scientist with their role as political participant and policy advisor, it is worth emphasizing that the role of social scientists in doing research about policy effects is exactly parallel to the role of natural scientists in doing their empirical research. This research is descriptive and predictive rather than prescriptive and normative. It is the factual study of what is rather than the evaluative study of what should be. As Max Weber painstakingly explained more than half a century ago, factual research is by no means value free. "The choice of the object of investigation and the extent or depth to which investigation attempts to penetrate into the infinite casual web, are determined by the evaluative ideas which dominate the investigator and his age" (Shils and Finch 1949:84). However, although the choice of topic and depth of study are subjective, the methods and results of factual study are objective in the sense that they are not "valid for one person and not others" but rather they are "valid for all who seek the truth."

Thus, the results of scientific research should be valid for all the various parties interested in environmental decisionmaking—in Congress, other agencies, state and local government, business, labor, public interest groups, academia, and the general public—regardless of their preferences, moral values, political beliefs, or ideological perspectives. A good piece of policy analysis, on the other hand, will incisively and concisely focus on the particular concerns of a specific decisionmaker.

Scientific Research Other than Research on Effects

Most scientists are not only parochial in their views about the nature and range of policy-relevant research on health effects, economic effects, social effects, and so on, but they also fail to appreciate that three other kinds of research can be as useful to policymakers in setting environmental standards as research on effects. This blindness is reflected in the fact that virtually none of EPA's internal research or sponsored research lies in these three areas. Indeed, little research is being conducted in these areas by anyone anywhere. Consequently, a few dollars of research support—by EPA, the National Science Foundation (NSF), other agencies, or private foundations—in these three areas will almost surely yield disproportionately large harvests.

The three areas involve assessment, research about preferences, and research about policy design. Figure 5-4 lays out the relationships of these kinds of research to each other, to scientific research about effects, and to policy analysis.

Figure 5-4. A Decomposition of Roles in Environmental Standard-Setting from a Policy Analysis Perspective.

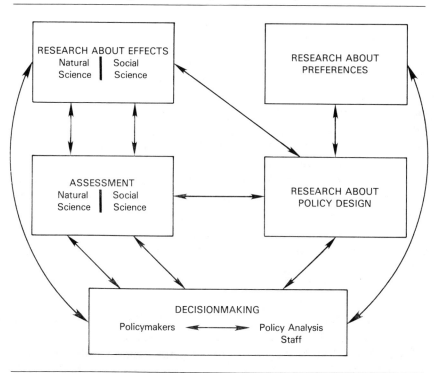

Assessment. The need for assessment arises because often the various facts uncovered by natural science and social science research are only indirectly relevant to the decision at hand, are in partial conflict with other facts, and are not sufficient or well enough established to remove uncertainty. For instance, evidence may be available about the effect of high doses of some environmental pollutant on rats, whereas the decisionmaker is concerned about the effect of low doses on humans. A number of rat experiments may have been done, some showing little or no effect while others show a subtantial effect. Evidence from epidemiological investigations of human populations may be so weak as to only suggest a wide probability distribution on the possible effects. Experts may have formed judgments about the possible effects, formed not on the basis of some single, objective experiment, but on the basis of their wide experience with related phenomena. These judgments, although subjective, may be highly informative. Consequently, assessment involves the synthesis of disparate and indirectly relevant evidence, both objective and judgmental, in order to assess estimates or probability distributions of the quantities of primary concern in the decision problem. Assessment is not a substitute for evidence, but rather a systematic synthesis of the available evidence. Although assessment is partially judgmental, the judgment here is scientific rather than moral or political. Thus, like scientific research, assessments should (given this definition) be valid for all parties concerned about environmental policymaking.

The process of eliciting scientific judgments, of synthesizing these judgments with the available array of disparate and indirectly relevant information, and of expressing the results, when necessary, in probabilistic terms requires specialized skills and methods that have largely been developed (to the extent they have as yet been developed) by mathematical statisticians, decision analysts, and cognitive psychologists.[8] That the methods of assessment are, as yet, weak, that few people understand them, and that a great deal of research, development, and training is required cannot be denied. In any logical scheme of environmental policy analysis, however, it is undeniable that the assessment phase plays a crucial role. Whether done well or poorly, assessment must be done, even if it simplistically involves selecting the *best* study and making some extrapolations from it.

Since James Ware's chapter in this volume focuses on the methods of assessment, it is not necessary to review those methods here. Nonetheless, the task of assessment is so crucial and so neglected that it seems appropriate to briefly point out four especially important but largely unrecognized research needs.

First, as indicated in Figure 5-4, assessment is required not only for natural science facts but also for social science facts, such as, for example, the cost of a regulation. Much of what research is being done to develop better methods of assessment focuses on natural science assessment. Parallel research is needed on social science assessment.

Second, given that decisionmakers do not want to be inundated with information, a key set of issues in assessment involves how to aggregate and summarize information, including:

- how to summarize over different kinds of health and nonhealth effects (e.g., over different states of morbidity);
- how to summarize over effects on different individuals;
- how to aggregate and synthesize different experts' judgments;
- how to indicate the range of uncertainty;
- how to indicate the volatility of the estimates (i.e., how much new information might change the estimates); and
- how to indicate the degree of expert confidence, consensus, and disagreement.

Third, beyond the fact that policymakers tend to be busy, they also have limited cognitive abilities. For example, some policymakers may not have a good intuitive feel for what a gamma distribution with a shape parameter of 2 and a scale parameter of 3.5 looks like. Thus, in addition to pruning and synthesizing information, an assessment should present information in a way that is meaningful and intelligible to the intended audience. Tables 5-1 and 5-2 illustrate one way to present information in a simple way on the morbidity effects of three alternative environmental standards. The tables are not intended as examples to be followed, but rather as examples of how much synthesis and simplification might be required to make the available information useful to a decisionmaker.

Fourth and finally, although an important and widely used approach to the task of assessment is to convene a panel of experts—for example, an NAS committee or a panel of EPA's Scientific Advisory Board—little is known about how to bring out the best of an expert committee. The internal dynamics of group behavior coupled with external pressures can lead to group reports that fail to capture the various experts' true judgments, uncertainties, and disagreements

Table 5-1.   How Many People Will be Affected under Alternative Standards?

	Percentage of U.S. Population Suffering One or More EDRAs[a] Per Year		Percentage of Most Sensitive 1 Percent of U.S. Population Suffering One or More EDRAs Per Year	
Standard	Best Estimate (%)	98% Credence Range	Best Estimate (%)	98% Credence Range
A	5	1–30	20	3–50
B	9	2–41	35	5–62
C	12	4–49	50	10–74

[a]EDRA, equivalent day of restricted activity.

about these judgments. It would be useful to do research on how an appropriate staff could be trained to help expert committees better understand the statistical methodology of assessment, the intricacy and subtlety involved in the elicitation of judgments, and the peculiar patterns of group behavior.

It would be highly productive for EPA to devote a small fraction of its research budget—a few million dollars a year, say—to research on these four issues in assessment, as well as to some of the statistical issues discussed in James Ware's chapter. Even when natural science and social science facts are plentiful, if these facts and resulting scientific judgments are not synthesized and presented adequately, decisionmakers are forced to make their choice in a fog of confusion and ignorance.

Research about Preferences.   Although neglected, objective research about subjective preferences, including ethical beliefs, political judgments, and ideological perspectives, is not a paradox but an activity highly useful and relevant to policymaking. The two fundamental sources of complexity and controversy in making environmental decisions are pervasive uncertainty and perplexing tradeoffs. The tradeoff problem is probably the more basic problem since continuing scientific research will tend to reduce the uncertainties and, in so doing, clarify—and hence heighten—realization of the competition between different objectives. Even if there were no uncertainty

Table 5-2. How Much Will People Be Affected Under
Alternative Standards?

	Average Number of EDRAs[a] Per Year Suffered by U.S. Population		Average Number of EDRAs Per Year Suffered by Most Sensitive 1 Percent of U.S. Population	
Standard	Best Estimate	98% Credence Range	Best Estimate	98% Credence Range
A	0.3	0.1–0.8	2.3	0.4–5.2
B	0.6	0.2–1.0	3.9	0.6–6.5
C	0.8	0.4–1.2	5.7	1.1–7.8

[a]EDRA, equivalent day of restricted activity.

and the future could be foretold perfectly, decisionmakers would still have to wrestle with such puzzling questions as:

- How much of our limited resources should be allocated to lifesaving activities versus other pressing social concerns?
- How important is the psychological well-being associated with clean air and blue skies?
- How much weight should be placed on an asthma attack suffered by a thirty-year old compared with a bout of emphysema suffered by a sixty-year old?
- How should our society react to saving the lives of one hundred Americans a millennium from now versus one hundred starving Africans today?
- Do we have the responsibility for maintaining ecological balances for nature's sake rather than, or in addition to, man's sake?
- Should we as a society be willing to impose costs and risks on a few members of society in order to benefit most members of society?
- What are the occasions for which paternalism is a legitimate stance for governmental agencies?

Since questions like these complicate all important environmental decisions, it is absolutely clear that there can never be an objectively scientific method for environmental decisionmaking.[9] Nevertheless, researchers may be able to help policymakers grapple with tradeoff problems in several ways.

First, researchers can trace out the consequences of adherence to different systems of preferences and values. More specifically, they can formulate persuasive systems of ethical axioms and then logically derive various normative conclusions. Three recent and widely read philosophical books, by Rawls (1971), Nozick (1974), and Ackerman (1980), do this starting from three different sets of basic axioms. Second, researchers can check for consistency and coherence between different ethical beliefs. In particular, they can check whether or not some normative position (e.g., all carcinogens should be banned) is consistent with another ethical belief (e.g., that no policy should be undertaken that makes the least privileged group in society even less privileged). Arrow's (1951) impossibility theorem is a famous example of this line of research. Third, researchers can describe and measure how various people view specific tradeoff problems, for example, how much the general public and different interest groups are willing to pay for some aspect of environmental quality (Freeman 1979). Fourth, researchers can develop methods to facilitate the sharing of different points of view among the various parties interested in some policy problem. Fifth, researchers can develop formal analytical methods for structuring tradeoff problems. The most notable example here is Keeney and Raiffa's (1976) book, *Decisions with Multiple Objectives: Preferences and Value Tradeoffs.*

One of the principle sources of the difficulty that natural scientists have in comprehending the nature of rational environmental decisionmaking is that most natural scientists have not been educated to think seriously and systematically about tradeoffs. Sometimes scientific tradeoff problems arise—between doing two cheaper experiments or one better one; between undertaking a well-trodden line of research almost certain to produce relatively dull results versus undertaking a risky experiment that might lead to reknown; between a simpler theory and one that better explains the data; or between an explanation that is consistent with the main body of theory in a discipline versus one that explains the data better but is inconsistent with the established wisdom. But these tradeoffs are rarely confronted explicitly. They are made more or less intuitively, and the focus of the scientist's attention is on the single objective of expanding the realm of the known. Given the great influence of scientists on environmental decisionmaking, it might be useful for some research to be funded—perhaps by NSF or a private foundation—on how to better educate and inform scientists about the nature of and necessity for tradeoffs.

Research about Policy Design.   A diverse array of strategies can be employed to cope with health, safety, and environmental hazards, including:

- medical care,
- insurance,
- consumer demand,
- regulatory standards or bans,
- labelling,
- tort liability,
- tax penalties,
- restrictions on behavior,
- collective bargaining,
- effluent fees,
- personal protective action,
- economic progress,
- biomedical research,
- safety engineering research, and
- risk analysis research.

Although each of these strategies is, on occasion, useful, all of them suffer from serious limitations and deficiencies. Consequently, it is useful to try to devise improved strategies, including better variations of existing strategies and multiple, combined strategies.

Architecture and engineering demonstrate that the endeavor of design is a complicated but rewarding pursuit. It is surprising, then, that policy design, as an analytical pursuit in its own right, has been so neglected, although some politicians, arbitrators, and mediators have acquired great skill at it. In any case, policy design is conceptually different from the other tasks diagrammed in Figure 5-4.

Policy design starts with an understanding of why various given alternatives are relatively strong or weak along different dimensions. Such understanding fuels creativity about devising new alternatives. The understanding of pros and cons can be gained, in part, by listening carefully to the various points of view expressed in a policy debate. Since these points of view are seldom diametrically opposed with equal and opposite weight given to all objectives, it is often possible to design solutions that go considerably further than halfway in meeting each interested group's desires and demands. The policy debate might not thereby be resolved, but instead of a raging dispute between lackluster policy alternatives A and B, the debate could be raised to a more cordial disagreement between the innovative and superior alternatives C and D.[10]

Interactions Among Roles

Two-way communication will clearly be required among individuals engaged in the various roles sketched above and in Figure 5-4. If scientists are to provide policymakers with relevant factual information—whether about natural science effects, social science effects, or preferences—they have to have some idea of what the policymakers' interests are. This is even more true for the assessors and for the policy designers who serve as bridges between the research community and the policy community. To the extent, however, that the reported results of the scientific endeavors of research and assessment become distorted by scientists' subjective preferences about the social good and the public interest, they will cease to be the descriptive and objective truths that constitute science.

Scientific experts cannot and should not be disenfranchised from the political process. They hold value opinions and are entitled to be heard. Indeed, it can be argued that scientists who can understand the biological, physical, or economic subtleties of complex policy questions have a special obligation to serve society by speaking out on controversial issues. Such scientists do society and the endeavor of science a disservice, however, if they fail to try to make clear where their scientific expertise ends and their nonexpert value judgments begin. Otherwise, in the short run their personal opinions will receive too much weight and, in the long run, scientific research will become tainted, mistrusted, and discounted.[11]

CONCLUDING OBSERVATIONS

Of the variety of points made in this chapter (which might be subtitled "Modestly and Conditionally Prescriptive Musings about Some Vast Questions of Institutional Design"), two seem worthy of special emphasis: First, three categories of research that could substantially improve the quality of environmental decisionmaking are woefully neglected. These research categories are assessment, research on preferences, and research on policy design. Second, scientific research and policy analysis are so profoundly different that most scientists (both natural and social) have little understanding of the nature of policy analysis. Scientists would be wise to be more reticent about making unconditional policy pronouncements *ex cathedra*. Furthermore, scientific research should not be confused with or considered a substitute for policy analysis. Policy analysis should be recognized as a distinctive and important endeavor, and the capability of EPA to do policy analysis should be strengthened.

NOTES

1.   Although this chapter focuses on standard-setting by the Environmental Protection Agency, much of the discussion also applies to such health and safety agencies as the Food and Drug Administration, Occupational Safety and Health Administration, Consumer Product Safety Commission, Nuclear Regulatory Commission, National Highway Traffic Safety Administration, and Federal Aviation Administration.

2.   Clean Air Act, 42 U.S.C. 740 *et seq.*, 1970, amended 1977, Section 109(b)(1).

3.   Clean Air Act, Section 112(b)(1)(B).

4.   Resource Conservation and Recovery Act, 42 U.S.C. 6921 *et seq.* 1976; and Solid Waste Disposal Act, 42 U.S.C. 6901 *et seq.* 1976, amended 1978.

5.   For a comparison of "risk only," "technology bases," and "balancing" statutes, see Regulatory Council (1979).

6.   Federal Water Pollution Control Act, 33 U.S.C. 1251 *et seq.* 1972, amended 1977; and Clean Air Act, Section III.

7.   As part of my work as study director of the National Academy of Sciences' Committee on Risk and Decision Making, I asked scores of scientists and analysts to suggest research topics.

8.   The best source of recent thinking is: Environmental Protection Agency (1981).

9.   For an extended discussion, see Shils and Finch (1949).

10.   For an excellent example of research on policy design, see Chapter 7.

11.   This paragraph is based on an unpublished draft report prepared by the Committee on Risk and Decision Making of the National Academy of Sciences (1981).

REFERENCES

Ackerman, Bruce. 1980. *Social Justice in the Liberal State.* New Haven: Yale University Press.

Arrow, Kenneth J. 1951. *Social Choice and Individual Values.* New York: John Wiley & Sons.

Committee on Risk and Decision Making of the National Academy of Sciences. 1981. Unpublished draft report.

Environmental Protection Agency. 1981. "Six Conceptual Risk Assessment Approaches." Research Triangle Park, N.C.: Office of Air Quality Planning and Standards (June).

Freeman, A. Myrick. 1979. *The Benefits of Environmental Improvement.* Baltimore: Johns Hopkins Press.

Keeney, Ralph L., and Howard Raiffa. 1976. *Decisions with Multiple Objectives: Preferences and Value Tradeoffs.* New York: John Wiley & Sons.

Moore, Mark H. 1980. "Social Science and Policy Analysis: Some Fundamental Differences." Unpublished paper, Harvard University (November 26).

Nozick, Robert. 1974. *Anarchy, State, and Utopia.* New York: Basic Books.

Rawls, John. 1971. *A Theory of Justice.* Cambridge: Harvard University Press.

Regulatory Council. 1979. "Statement on Regulation of Chemical Carcinogens." *Federal Register* 44 (October 17):60038.

Shils, Edward A., and Henry A. Finch, eds. 1949. *Max Weber on the Methodology of the Social Sciences.* Glencoe, Ill.: The Free Press.

6 SOME PROBLEMS OF IMPLEMENTING MARKETABLE POLLUTION RIGHTS SCHEMES: THE CASE OF THE CLEAN AIR ACT

Marc J. Roberts

Economists have long been advocates of markets and marketlike mechanisms as an alternative to "command and control" regulation for accomplishing public purposes. Such advocacy has nowhere been more intensive and extensive than concerning the possible use of "effluent fees" or "marketable pollution rights" as an approach to environmental problems.[1] Perhaps as a result, in recent years there have been several policy developments that embody various aspects of these ideas. Especially notable among them are the "tradeoff" and "bubble" policies developed by the previous administration within the framework of the Clean Air Act.[2]

The purpose of this chapter is to examine how these policies—seen as steps toward a marketable pollution rights regime—have worked out in practice. We examine the following questions: To what extent do the models and arguments used by economists to justify such policies capture the important aspects of real situations? What features of a particular problem make the analysis more applicable, thus making

The research underlying this paper was made possible by a grant from the Sloan Foundation to the Harvard School of Public Health. I gratefully acknowledge the help and advice of my colleague Stephen Thomas, whose work on the Sohio case was critical to the development of many of the arguments herein.

93

marketable rights schemes easier to implement? Where there are implementation difficulties, how can these kinds of schemes be modified to make them more effective? In particular, when and where are more complete market systems (such as that proposed by Hahn and Noll elsewhere in this volume) attractive alternatives to the current approach? Finally, since the way we formulate our national air quality goals has such serious implications for how such schemes operate, what does consideration of these issues tell us about the extent to which such standards should take into account the costs as well as the benefits of air quality improvements?

The gods have been unkind enough to confront us with some difficult problems. The real world is, alas, much more complex than the hypothetical world economists usually consider when they argue for marketable pollution rights schemes. As a result, those arguments have often failed to grapple with a host of complex issues. Consideration of those issues suggests that any real marketable permit scheme will be a crude, nonoptimal compromise precisely because a more finely-tuned scheme will often carry with it prohibitively high transaction and knowledge costs. Furthermore, the interests of buyers and sellers in such markets will be unusually aligned. Under some circumstances they will have a mutual incentive to overstate what the seller has conveyed to the buyer. As a result, natural market antagonism will not necessarily operate to discipline market participants and much of the burdensome enforcement process associated with current regulation will have to remain in place.

If marketable permit schemes are to offer meaningful reductions in the costs of pollution control, we must solve two problems. First, we must find ways to lower the transaction costs to participants in these markets. Second, we must be able to formulate more adequately and to make explicit decisions about the kinds of environmental risks we are willing to accept. To do the former, we must often also do the latter. But before discussing such conclusions, let us review the history to date.

BACKGROUND

The intellectual origins of the notion that economic incentives can be used to regulate the undesirable side effects of productive activities are obscure. The scheme is clearly present in Pigou's (1932) *Economics of Welfare,*[3] in which he suggests that the notion is in turn traceable to Marshall. In the post World War II period, Allen Kneese and various associates at Resources for the Future played a major role in establishing effluent fees as the accepted orthodox policy.[4] Furthermore, the effluent fees approach complements the intellectual structure economists use to analyze various policy problems. General equilibrium theory purports to show how perfectly competitive markets can produce the sort of efficient (Pareto optimal) outcomes that economists now largely accept as an appropriate normative reference point for public policy.[5] I have argued elsewhere (Roberts 1972) that there are real limitations to such a normative standard, but that is not at issue at this point. Market resource allocation processes within such a model are guided by prices—the "invisible hand" that tells producers what to produce and buyers what to buy and guides firms to utilize efficient combinations of inputs. Market failures of various sorts lead to "wrong" prices (Bator 1958); hence the injunction to correct such mistakes by setting the "right" prices through fees or taxes seems self-evident.

The environment is often seen as a prime example of such market failure. No one owns the environment so no one can charge for its use. Also, many are affected by environmental quality and it would be costly to organize them to pay for what they enjoy, or to prevent them from enjoying it if they refused to pay.[6] Because of these structural difficulties, the argument goes, the potential buyers of cleanup cannot organize themselves to pay the possible sellers of cleanup (i.e., polluters) a price equal to the value of such cleanup to the buyers. Why not, then, intervene to set the right prices! Charge polluters for waste discharged into the air or water, using the incentives of the competitive economy to correct the problem at hand.

Unfortunately, it has been difficult to convince anyone but economists to take such effluent fee schemes seriously. Lawmakers, frequently lawyers by background, have found it difficult to accept using the market to achieve socially desirable results (Roberts 1980). In the air pollution area especially, the rationale for the pollution control program is the achievement of ambient standards designed to protect human health. Critics of effluent fees ask whether we could afford the risk that large firms would respond irrationally by paying the fees rather than paying the lower costs of abatement.

Some environmentalists also contend that it is symbolically inappropriate to allow some firms to buy a "license to pollute." Many congressmen voted for the Clean Air Act on the assumption that pollution, any pollution, was and should be treated as a crime, and that one does not sell licenses to allow people to engage in illegal acts. Doing so undermines the moral sanction on such conduct and hence the political and social basis for controlling it.

Oft-repeated assurances from economists (Kneese and Schultze 1975) about how firms will rationally try to reduce costs and will clean up if cleanup is cheaper than the fee, and their suggestion that it is better to sell such licenses than to give them away, have not been persuasive. Occasionally, isolated lawmakers have introduced such legislation. The "Coalition to Tax Pollution" interested one subcommittee in holding hearings on a "sulfur tax" bill,[7] but on this point the economics profession has been virtually talking to itself throughout most of the environmental boom of the 1970s.

Meanwhile, almost unnoticed, another idea was making its way into the literature. In 1968, John Dales advocated the establishment of real licenses to pollute—marketable pollution rights that each source would have to purchase and that would constrain the quantity of pollution it could add to an ecosystem. About the same time in England, Mishan (1969) put forward the similar idea of "amenity rights" (to quiet and light) that would-be polluters would be required to purchase from existing owners. Then in an important and, as far as I know, unpublished paper, Jacoby and Schaumberg (1965) showed how a stock of licenses could be set for a river in order to guarantee the maintenance of a target minimum level of environmental quality, defined as the level of dissolved oxygen at the point of worst conditions along the river.[8] Their scheme requires that rights for discharging organic material at different points along the river be tradable at rates that reflect the relative impact of the discharges on conditions in the so-called critical reach.

These results were extended by Montgomery (1972) to an air pollution example. Assuming a deterministic, linear model of the impact of pollution discharges on air pollution levels, he showed that to achieve ambient air quality for "m" substances at "n" points logically requires "n" times "m" sets of licenses. More recently, Roberts and Spence (1976) and Weitzman (1974) have shown that rights schemes are especially attractive in the presence of nonlinear damage functions of the "threshold" sort. In the presence of uncertainty about the costs of control, rights schemes allow one to determine output quantities, although marginal control costs are not perfectly predictable.

In contrast, if pollution sources are rational, a fee scheme allows a policymaker to set a limit on the marginal costs of pollution control all sources will undertake, but leaves the ultimate environmental conditions imperfectly specified.

Rights schemes have apparently been more politically acceptable than fees because they directly limit how much pollution will occur. Moreover, they can, with some struggle, be fit into the framework of the Clean Air Act. There have also been some attempts to utilize marketable rights in state water pollution control plans,[9] but it is under the Clean Air Act that the most significant developments have occurred.

The Clean Air Act requires the states to determine the level of emissions consistent with nationally uniform ambient air quality standards for various pollutants. These standards are determined by the EPA administrator. Each state must proclaim the necessary regulations to achieve these standards through what are called State Implementation Plans, or SIPs. The first movement toward a marketable rights scheme occurred when EPA encountered the problem of whether or not it could allow states to allow new facilities to locate in areas that were in violation of the national standards. The Clean Air Act requires that SIPs insure "reasonable further progress" toward compliance with those standards. How could allowing new sources to produce additional pollution in already dirty areas be made consistent with that injunction?

The case that raised the issue in an unavoidable way was the proposal by the Sohio Company to expand the terminal facilities at Long Beach, California in order to import Alaskan oil (Thomas 1980: Chapters 6,7). Long Beach is located within the Los Angeles area, an air basin in serious violation of ambient air quality standards. Yet at a time of energy crisis with much hope for Alaskan oil as a contributor to energy independence, how was EPA to refuse to allow the new facility be built? In part to avoid this dilemma and in response to other proposals on the horizon, in December of 1976 EPA issued an Interpretive Ruling which specified that a new facility could be built provided that the new source somehow induced old sources to decrease their pollution by more than the new source added.[10] Thus growth was made compatible with progress toward attainment. Many detailed issues remained to be resolved; nevertheless, by asking new sources in nonattainment areas to secure tradeoffs, the potential for a market in pollution rights had been created. (The Clean Air Act Amendments of 1977 have since codified the policy as an option under the law.)[11]

The bubble policy is directed at existing as opposed to new sources, but like the tradeoff policy, it evolved from EPA's efforts to deal with specific cases. There had been early discussions of the bubble idea in connection with nonferrous smelting facilities, but that did not lead to any new policies. More recently, the bubble approach grew out of a series of steel industry enforcement negotiations which EPA had decided to handle centrally. (Since many of the companies operated in more than one EPA region, the usual practice of allowing regional offices to negotiate threatened inconsistency and weakened EPA's negotiating position.) Several steel firms were confronted with very high control costs for eliminating particulate emissions from certain sources. At the same time they believed that there were other sources within their plants from which such reductions could be obtained at lower cost. Drawing upon earlier agency thinking, both sides agreed on a way to achieve such cost savings. Once emissions limits were defined for each source, a bubble would be placed over the facility. Compliance would be determined on the basis of the total emissions within the bubble, not on a process-by-process basis. More recently, through regulation, EPA recognized the possibility of interplant bubbles and yet another potential market for pollution rights was created.

IMPLEMENTING THE TRADEOFF AND BUBBLE POLICIES

By the spring of 1981, four years after the tradeoff policy went into effect, there appear to have been over a thousand instances of permits having been issued under the regulations.[12] However, for all but thirty-five or so facilities, these have been "internal" offsets—reductions provided by a firm for its own activities. Furthermore, in all but nine or ten cases the "external" offsets were not in fact cash transactions. Instead, they were donated by state and local governments or by cooperating or failing firms. The bubble policy, having been in effect for a shorter time, has so far produced only a few completed applications, none of which was for an interfirm transaction.

This record hardly suggests that the use of marketable pollution rights has swept the nation. To be sure, every transaction may involve worthwhile real resource savings, but many economists, including the author, have argued that the potential cost-savings from redistributing the burden of pollution control should be relatively great due to the highly unequal marginal control costs under the current regulatory regime. If that is so, why have there not been more transactions? Furthermore, why has there been so much criticism of both of these policy initiatives from both industry and environmentalists?

What Can be Traded for What?

In order for any offset or interplant bubble transaction to be consummated, it is necessary to determine: how much pollution the new source will emit, the decrease in the emissions of existing ("seller") sources, and whether or not the pollution reduction can be traded for the pollution from the new source. Yet each of these steps may involve many detailed and vexatious definitional questions that often have significant policy implications.

When economists discuss such matters they sometimes talk as if monitoring devices were available to cheaply and reliably record the amount of all pollution emissions. If that were the case, decisions about whether a source had curtailed its pollution by the promised amount and whether a new source was emitting no more than the tradeoff transaction implied could be left to straightforward data gathering by an enforcement agent. Unfortunately, such monitoring devices typically are not available and enforcement authorities know they will not be able to monitor compliance well, so they must decide what tradeoffs to allow on the basis of forecasts of what the buyers and sellers in the tradeoff transaction will emit. This means they have to forecast not only the effectiveness of the pollution control measures each will install, but also the operating rates, operating hours, product mixes, and input mixes of the various participants in the transaction. In the Sohio case, for example, there was much dispute over the amount of hydrocarbon emissions from old tanks as opposed to the new tanks that were to replace them.

In addition, one needs to decide which of the changes in the pollution levels caused by a project are to be counted as within the scope of the project. Consider pollution from workers' cars, from trucks and boats delivering and taking away products, and from electricity generated for the new facility. Are these to be emissions against which offsets are to be required? In the Sohio case the questions of how to count tanker emissions and whether or not to count increased utility emissions arguably associated with the project were notably difficult to answer. How close did the tankers have to be to Long Beach before their emissions counted? Did one count only engine and normal fuel tank emissions or did one also allow for evaporation from oil discharged in either routine ballasting or accidental spills?

To the extent that we can design a system that is relatively comprehensive, such scope problems will tend to disappear. All discharges or changes in discharges—even presumably motor vehicle emissions—would then belong to someone and would be constrained by their permit conditions. However, in the real world we are far from such a system. Sources are numerous and for many, emissions are either small or difficult to determine (e.g., hydrocarbons from highway surfaces or from housepainters), or they are mobile (e.g., tankers). Hence it may be very expensive and perhaps impractical to construct a comprehensive permit system. This may make the notion of marketable permits much more applicable when only a relatively small number of large sources is involved. (Note that Hahn and Noll deal with this problem by shifting the emissions license burden from motor vehicle owners to fuel refiners in order to restrict the number of permit holders to a manageably small number. They do not consider, however, what this will do to barriers to entry and to general competitive conditions in regional gasoline markets.)

Finally, even if one has solved these problems, another troublesome definitional issue remains, namely, how to decide if two emission sources offset each other. One part of this question is a matter of the physical and biochemical characteristics of the traded emissions. For example, if we are trading particulates, are they similar in the extent to which they contain the smaller size respirable particles that are thought to be especially harmful? Likewise, are the two sources similar in the toxicity of their emissions? This has been a major issue in some steel industry bubble proposals.

A second aspect of comparability is the geographic location of the two sources. Particularly for total suspended particulate matter (TSP) and sulfur dioxide (SO_2), patterns of diffusion are such that under most atmospheric conditions emissions form distinguishable plumes downwind for many miles. Suppose the old and the new source are a few miles apart, or their stacks are of different heights, or their stack gases are of different temperatures or exit velocities. Under many meteorological conditions the area whose air quality is being improved by the added controls on one source will not coincide (or perhaps only coincide partially) with the region whose air quality is being deteriorated by the new source. For example, in some offset transactions pollution reductions have been obtained by resurfacing roads with a water-based compound to curtail the hydrocarbon emissions from petroleum-based solvents. How far away from a new plant should such resurfacing be allowed to count? In at least one case, some of the resurfacing occurred more than 50 miles from the new facility.

There is also the question of the time phasing of curtailments and new emissions. Suppose peak hydrocarbon evaporation from the unresurfaced roads mentioned above occurs in the spring or summer, while peak emissions from the new manufacturing plant occur in the fall? Similarly, in the Sohio case, at the urging of the state regulators, Southern California Edison agreed to install a scrubber on a power plant to reduce emissions. Again, how likely are the new emissions and the curtailment to coincide over time?

While I offer some thoughts in the next section about how some of these difficulties might be dealt with, the more general issues are quite clear. The more broadly we define the zone of acceptable substitutions, the more risk we run that the resulting trades might produce some deterioration in environmental quality because of geographic or temporal "bunching," or the substitution of more harmful for less harmful emissions. (Of course, trades might coincidentally happen to make things better as well as worse.) If we try to deal with such worries by ad hoc review, we are likely to significantly increase the time and resources required for each transaction, as well as the uncertainty of potential participants. If we try to specify rules or side conditions to limit such potential harm or create multiple permits, we may unduly complicate the market or restrict the number of potential participants in any one trade so that the market becomes too cumbersome or thin to operate. Such difficulties are surely more serious in some situations than in others, so the attractiveness of controlled trading may be dependent upon the detailed technical features of each situation—a conclusion that is, if nothing else, psychologically unappealing to many in its lack of generality or theoretical elegance.

There are several points to be drawn from this recitation of definitional difficulties. The first is that under current arrangements a great deal of scientific and administrative work needs to be done to define the terms of each bubble or offset transaction. These are not standardized commodities like wheat futures contracts that can be bought and sold with minimum transaction costs. There are many markets for complex commodities in the world (e.g., baseball teams, shopping malls, or computer companies). However, such markets are unlikely to be perfect and transaction costs tend to be high. The extent to which government action can lower those costs and thereby encourage transactions may be critical to the actual success of the policy and to the number of trades that eventually occur.

There is an added complication here, however. Unlike many transactions that are self-policing in that buyer and seller interests are opposed, in offset transactions both buyer and seller have an incentive to overstate the amount of reduction being transferred. A somewhat analogous situation is the tactic of overstating the value of a nursing home in a non-arms-length transaction with a cooperative buyer in order to increase the cost basis of the ultimate owner for reimbursement purposes. Given this mutual incentive of buyers and sellers to exaggerate the actual emission reductions, and given our limited ability to measure these reductions, it is likely that for each transaction there will continue to be the need for substantial involvement in and approval by a public agency. Pollution rights markets are unlikely to be the smoothly working, privately operated, multiparty impersonal arenas economists usually have in mind when they call something a market. Instead, most pollution rights markets will have many of the features of current regulation. Such schemes may well allow waste sources the possibility of making cost-reducing counter-proposals as to how the burden of cleanup might be distributed and this may well be desirable. But let us not be mislead by calling the result a market. A more refined terminology is called for. A man who says only "feline" and thus does not differentiate between alley cats and bengal tigers may be seriously mislead by the failure of his categories to make relevant distinctions.

Who Has What Rights?

Many of our current difficulties on this question arise because we do not have a comprehensive system of discharge permits that specify allowable discharge quantities, unlike, say, the scheme Hahn and Noll propose. Instead, we have effectively distributed rights equal to current emissions. But what are current emissions for this purpose? Firms are required to achieve certain rates of pollution control, or of emissions, as specified by SIPs or their discharge permits. As a result, variations in hours of operation, production rates, product mix or inputs can all effect a source's air pollution emissions. What assumptions do we make in computing a source's available emissions rights?

If we try to assign rights directly, as Hahn and Noll note, the initial distribution of rights may have serious implications for the nature and extent of the transactions that will occur in the market. Equally important are the wealth effects of any distribution scheme and its interaction with the politics of putting the policy into place. If rights are given to existing sources, their opposition to the scheme will be decreased. From that perspective, a pure auction of all rights seems politically infeasible. Yet if we are to encourage market activity, we cannot initially allocate all rights to those who most desire them, for if we do, no transactions will occur. Perhaps Dales' initial idea of designing the rights to be leases of varying terms, rather than perpetual (Hahn and Noll's assumption), might help "thicken" the market and let it display more informative price signals.

Nonperpetual rights also might help solve another problem with current rights assignment policies, namely, insuring the achievement of ambient air quality standards under the Clean Air Act. The current law envisages that states will undertake successive SIP revisions until attainment is achieved. But if a source's emissions rights equal its permitted discharges under the curent SIP, those emissions might become insulated from further restriction. Some environmentalists argue that this is especially worrisome because actual emissions are less than SIP allowable totals (due to lower production levels, more-than-required controls, etc.). They contend that creating a stock of permits equal to allowable emissions would lead to air quality deterioration. The problem is exacerbated because small sources and nonpoint sources now effectively escape the regulatory net. How can a rights market limit total emissions if small sources can be created and then become sellers without having been buyers when they came into existence?

This issue has come up in various guises. Should sources which close be allowed to sell their rights or should we use that occasion to squeeze slack out of the system? Should sources which were discharging less than they were permitted only be allowed to sell tradeoffs equal to actual emissions rather than permitted emissions? Environmentalists have taken a "use-it-or-lose-it" view that firms can only generate offsets by reducing emissions below those which they have emitted in the recent past, even if they might have legally emitted more due to, for example, higher output. They have argued that otherwise the trading policy will lead to "paper" offsets and an increase in actual pollution that will make it more difficult to move the regions in question toward attaining air quality standards. Advocates of trading have responded that the environmentalist approach penalizes those firms that have been conscientious or are in economic trouble, and discourages sources from cleaning up any more than they have to for fear of losing emissions rights. Similarly, the use-it-or-lose-it doctrine in water law leads to inefficient water resource use.[13]

This concern also supports opposition to the "banking" of emissions reductions (where a source cleans up now and sells reductions later) on the grounds that banked reductions might likewise be insulated from further regulatory tightening.[14] Finally, the need to move toward attainment has also been used to justify the requirement that tradeoff recipients in nonattainment areas install the most efficient possible control technology (LAER, or Lowest Achievable Emission Rate) regardless of how many permits they could or did acquire.[15]

Some years ago, Roberts and Stewart (1976) proposed one solution to this concern, namely, making all rights depreciable so that everyone expected, in advance, some steady tightening of the system. Dales' proposal that rights be created for varying terms could have a similar effect if the stock of rights were steadily contracted. Either approach, however, raises the more general dilemma that the more rights those who buy pollution rights are given, the less adjustable the system becomes from the viewpoint of public policy. Yet, if one makes these rights too imperfect, buyers and sellers will not be willing and able to trade them with confidence, and potential cost-reducing transactions will not occur. Indeed, the current rights seem so imperfect that several firms have suggested in interviews that they have kept dirty and inefficient facilities in operation longer than they otherwise would have. The predominant role of internal offsets suggests that this is not an isolated phenomenon.

The Distribution of Information and Transaction Costs

The extant mathematical models that relate pollution discharges to ambient air quality are typically expensive to implement as well as being poor descriptors of actual data. Even where extensive meteorological and air quality data are available and substantial ad hoc adjustment of the model to specific circumstances is undertaken, prediction errors of 50 percent to 150 percent are commonplace.[16] When the terrain is uneven or the meteorology complex, the models often do not work even this well. And sometimes the available air quality data is limited in both detail and duration, which makes the modeling effort still more problematical.

Given all these problems with modeling, there will generally be substantial uncertainty about the likely air quality impact of any proposed transaction in the market for air pollution rights. It is also quite difficult to determine exactly what stock of rights would be consistent with reliably attaining air quality goals. If we require too high a level of proof before we allow a transaction to take place, we may effectivley prevent any transactions from occurring. The requisite studies may well be so time-consuming and expensive as to absorb much of the potential gains from trade. Or they may be of such uncertain outcome that the sources involved decide it is not worthwhile to undertake them. Indeed, in the limiting case there may be no way at all to meet the requisite burden with our current intellectual technology.

Thus, designing any pollution market system requires a whole series of decisions as to who will bear what costs and burdens. How much monitoring (for how long, at how many sites and how sophisticated) will be required? What kinds of modeling must be done? Who will bear both the direct cost and the burden of the uncertainty? Are we going to ask sources to spend $10,000 to $50,000 up front and wait a year before we even begin to consider the transaction?

Given how poor the available pollution modeling techniques are, we also need to decide how tough to be. Are we prepared to say "no" to proposals that are marginally unacceptable on the basis of an admittedly crude model? If not, how far will we go? As in the case of how we define acceptable trades, this issue, too, involves a comparison between the risks of mistakes and the possible cost savings of a less constricted market. Nor is this just a hypothetical concern. It is apparent that the currently high transaction costs and the uncertain consequences of incurring those costs help to explain the low volume of interfirm transactions that have occurred to date.

Interestingly, under the Clean Air Act the most stringent modeling and monitoring requirements have been imposed not in connection with the tradeoff policy in nonattainment areas, but in connection with the PSD program (Goklany 1980). PSD stands for Prevention of Significant Deterioration and applies to new sources that want to locate in areas cleaner than the ambient standards. Such sources must demonstrate that their added emissions will not lead to a deterioration of ambient quality below allowable levels, which in many cases are more stringent than the primary standards. For just this reason industry is now generally urging a relaxation of such PSD procedures, and of the tradeoff and bubble procedures as well. But just how lax should various procedures be? How do we decide such questions?

Beyond some point the gains from better data and models may not be worth their costs. We are faced with a compromise among analytical sophistication, total cost, and the impact of that cost on the nature and volume of the transactions that will occur. In the next section I propose some ways to lower those costs because I believe we have not struck the appropriate compromise, but we cannot even discuss that issue until we go beyond the usual economists' enthusiasm for simple models.

Accountability and Enforceability

Once we have actually consummated a tradeoff transaction, our implementation problems are not yet over. Is the buyer of an offset responsible for insuring the seller's compliance with the deal, or does the seller's commitment become publicly enforceable? Given that the buyer would have little incentive to uncover a failure by the seller to curtail its pollution, seller responsibility and public enforcement directed at sellers would seem unavoidable. That does, however, further discourage sellers from selling. The need for such enforcement also moves us further toward a regulatory regime rather than toward a self-policing market. Indeed, it is not at all clear whether or not devices like offsets and the bubble policy will increase or decrease the need for regulatory agency expenditures.

Administrative Compatibility with the Clean Air Act

Implementing current rights schemes faces an additional problem, namely, the need to be compatible with the extant requirements of the Clean Air Act. The Act requires sources to agree to compliance schedules designed to attain air quality standards in time to meet statutory deadlines. Those source-by-source rules are considered part of the SIP and initially require case-by-case state and federal approval. On this basis, each and every transaction must undergo the notice, comment, and hearing requirements of the federal Administrative Procedure Act, even after they have satisfied whatever procedures the states require. Similarly, EPA initially took the position that an application by a firm to utilize the bubble policy could not be used as justification for relaxing any previously agreed upon schedule in the source's compliance plans. EPA's rationale was that, otherwise, spurious bubble applications might lead to widespread delay. Since some firms were facing the need to place orders for equipment which required long lead times in order to maintain schedules, those firms countered that they were being prevented from taking advantage of whatever savings the policy might offer by the need to proceed under the old rules.

Just before it left office, the previous EPA administration did promulgate new policies that partially responded to these problems.[17] The more general issue, however, is the extent to which one is prepared to take procedural shortcuts and enforcement risks in an attempt to implement an innovative policy. Does one truly want one or even two rounds of public hearings on each transaction? Is it a good idea to risk delay in reaching attainment in order to save costs, and how does one compare the probabilities and the magnitude of the effects in each instance? Again, pollution rights markets are not self-defining or self-implementing. Rather, they are inevitably embedded in a complex set of agency strategic calculations.

Interjurisdictional Effects

The conceptual framework of the marketable rights idea tends to be based on the assumption that air pollution occurs within a limited and well defined system. Indeed, the main body of the Clean Air Act is built upon the assumption that appropriate Air Quality Control Regions are of less-than-state scale. this may be fairly accurate in the case of the Los Angeles Basin, but it is seriously flawed if we are considering ozone in southeastern Connecticut or acid rain in upstate New York. In such cases the airshed is both ill-defined and certainly interstate. From a meteorological viewpoint, different geographic regions might even be appropriate as a basis for different air pollution rights markets, depending upon the atmospheric behavior of the pollutants in question. In addition, those boundaries are not likely to match existing administrative and political boundaries, so we are again likely to face a tradeoff between our capacity for fine-tuning a system and our need to insure effective management and to economize on limited political and administrative resources. This problem is not unique to a marketable rights approach. Any pollution control program has to deal with interjurisdictional effects, but using markets may well serve to highlight and focus increased attention on this issue, raising still another regulatory issue that must be decided in order to create the markets in question.

SOME IMPLICATIONS

I hope to have persuaded the reader that creating marketable permits for air pollution discharges is a difficult problem. As a long-time advocate of this approach, I have been taken aback by the many complexities I have uncovered. I remain convinced, however, that marketable rights schemes are promising, provided we view them cautiously and realistically. The key to making such a market work is to reduce the transaction costs to the participants and to widen the market to insure that there is a reasonable number of potential sellers for each buyer. Yet how can we accomplish these objectives and still insure that ambient standards will be achieved?

Ironically, many of our current difficulties are rooted in our unwillingness to more wholeheartedly embrace the marketable discharge permit idea. In particular, as long as we do not issue actual licenses, but instead create them implicitly through the tradeoff and bubble policies, we have to face the vexatious question of who has what rights. Should these be based on past emissions, permitted emissions, or likely future emissions? Also, what emissions count against a projected new activity? In a system where we had a complete and reliable emissions inventory and explicit permits for all sources, these questions would not arise. This suggests that if we are serious about trading, we should move in the direction of a full system of explicit permits. This conclusion is reinforced by the argument that movement toward attainment would be facilitated, not hindered, by such an approach if we had a depreciating or term permit system. For if we did have a complete license system, every source would be within the system of controls, and its costs (and hence its incentive to oppose progress) would be limited by the possibility of making cost-reducing trades.

Regardless of whether or not we do go that far, it would be helpful for the government to assume more of the modeling and monitoring costs of establishing these markets up front. For example, EPA might determine in advance, through its own analysis, how much emissions over each region in the country are acceptable, and allow all trades that satisfy those limits to occur without placing any burden of proof as to ambient consequences on would-be buyers and sellers. This procedure would drastically lower source-by-source modeling and monitoring requirements. Proposals now called "emission density zoning" are similar to this idea (EPA 1980). Of course, if the initial analysis is wrong or incomplete, the government may find it harder than under current practice to readjust the rules that it initially imposed. But I believe the gains of increased trade are worth these risks.

As to what can be traded for what, we must find ways to facilitate trades, rather than constantly worrying about avoiding all possible risks. And we must do so while making the rules simple and easy to follow. For example, if we believe that small particles are the most dangerous ones, then let us make these particles, rather than total particulates, the basis of the rules. Alternatively, we could specify ratios at which various types of particles (or other emissions) can be traded for one another. Or else we could simply ignore the issue on the grounds that we do not regulate small particles now and there is no reason to believe that, on average, a marketable permits scheme will be any worse in this respect.

The same considerations also apply to geographic coincidence issues. For reactive pollutants the problem is easier. Exactly because we do not know much about their atmospheric behavior, we can defensibly assume that emissions over a wide area are equivalent. This assumption, which implies a relatively wide market, is more or less the case Hahn and Noll considered, which suggests that marketable rights schemes are especially attractive in those instances. They may, for example, be useful as a way to control acid rain. If we want to limit certain emissions from the Ohio Valley to protect upstate New York and New England, we may be able to accept tradeoffs among many sources in the upwind states. Indeed, such a system could actually facilitate dealing with the interjurisdictional issues noted previously by placing a limit on total source-state emissions of concern to the receptor state.

For nonreactive pollutants, in order to broaden the geographic scope sufficiently, we may have to rethink what we mean by compliance with ambient standards. The lack of geographic coincidence of trading sources will inevitably lead to some geographic variations in ambient conditions, especially when we consider averaging times of less than a few days. In light of this prospect, one way to widen the scope of the market would be to allow some geographic averaging to be part of the definition of compliance with the standard, subject to some upper-bound constraints on how "hot" any ambient air quality "hot spot" could become. One rationale for such an approach would be to say that, in fact, the population damage function for air pollution is quite linear in the region of the standard, so that excesses in some areas can be appropriately balanced by better-than-standard conditions in others. Even if damage functions for individuals show clear thresholds, it seems likely that there is some distribution of those thresholds in the population as a function of differential sensitivity. Furthermore, the "adequate margin of safety" language in the Clean Air Act has lead to standards being set well below the threshold of the damage function of the bulk of the population. Thus, the situation might be like the one depicted in Figure 6-1. In the diagram, population damage is approximately linear in the region of the standard S because the population damage function does not become significantly nonlinear until the region in which most people are pushed across the thresholds of their individual damage functions.

The reasonability of this suggestion is reinforced by considering the (at best) probabilistic nature of compliance with any ambient standard. Current policies often ignore the fact that any given set of pollution discharges will give rise to a probability distribution of ambient quality. Instead, the early linear rollback analyses used to develop SIPs focused on the ratio of a worst case ambient level to the ambient standard and used that analysis to justify curtailing emissions in the same proportion. More recently, ambient standards have been written to incorporate an acceptable frequency of violation, which has in turn been interpreted as a probability of violation—a necessary step since a program which normally achieves a specified frequency of violations will occasionally do worse when conditions

Figure 6-1. Air Pollution Damage Function.

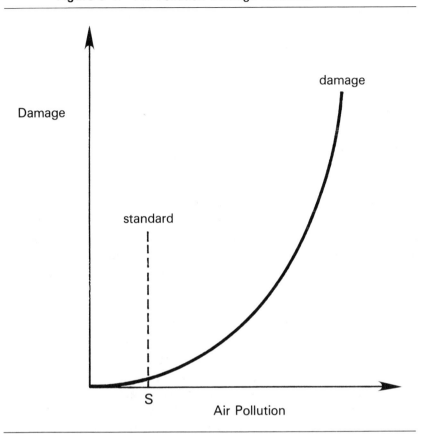

are adverse. What all this means, however, is that current policy already allows some violations of the standard. Thus, the question is whether or not we are willing to trade a higher probability of violation at some points for a lower probabilty at others. I see no way to create a wide enough tradeoff market without saying "yes" to this question, especially since current violation probabilities have been chosen quite arbitrarily without much evidence as to the health consequences of alternative probability levels.

More generally, in operating any tradeoff policy we will have to address explicitly the question of how unlikely a contingency must be before we no longer will spend resources to guard against it. What risks will we run with regard to unusual meteorology or to unlikely but possible operating conditions in order to decide what tradeoffs are necessary? In the Sohio case, for example, the environmentalists argued for enough controls to maintain air quality in cases where unusual meteorology, expectable only one day per year, and port operations, expectable one day per year, coincided—a probability of less than 1 in 100,000! The regulations, they claimed, required allowance for the worst case. Yet even this was not the worst case, as the rules did not cover the possibility of a simultaneous oil spill!

This last example illustrates the problem of time- phasing traded emissions. Even if the annual emissions achieved by a trade are acceptable, we may not want them bunched by unusual occurrences. This problem is obviously more acute when we are dealing with standards with shorter averaging times, since these standards are more likely to be violated by such bunching. In general, tradeoff rules do have to be specified in terms of limits on *emission rates per unit time,* and the time period that is appropriate is the same as that in the standard. Thus, if we care about annual exposures, permits should limit annual emissions. If short-term exposure matters, daily emissions must also be limited. And, as I noted some years ago (Roberts 1975), having short-term limits that vary seasonally, or even "on line" with ambient conditions, may be possible if the rules are simple enough.

How do we handle either low probability disasters or coincidences that might lead to much higher emissions for a short period? It seems foolish to try to deal with these problems by requiring purchasers to buy enough licenses to bring about sufficient emissions reductions to cover such contingencies. Instead, these problems call for specific rules designed to lower the risks of disasters, and perhaps some capacity to invoke additional restrictions when needed (along the lines of "smog alert" requirements).

Given that we do not achieve ambient standards with perfect reliability, perhaps the time has come to rethink how those standards should be set and what role they should play in our overall scheme. Are we prepared to insist upon the maintenance (or achievement) of such standards, even where doing so would imply extremely high marginal costs of control in some areas? Such a policy has potentially large distributive effects, such as creating rents for sources in regions where compliance is less expensive and encouraging industrial relocation toward such regions.

Perhaps in part for this reason, several state air pollution control agency directors from industrial states have been pushing for a change to nationally uniform technology-based discharge standards for existing sources. Similarly, industries which believe they have few choices about facility location (e.g., oil drillers) are becoming concerned whether or not under a permit system any permits will be available to allow them to expand their activities in some areas.

From an economist's usual viewpoint, nationally uniform technology-based standards are difficult to justify, but nationally uniform ambient standards are not much better. Is it likely that the marginal costs and benefits of pollution control will be equal either at the same marginal cost level or at the same ambient level in the highly varied situations we find across the nation? Health benefits will vary with population, control costs will vary with industrial development, and some regions are aesthetically more valuable than others. Indeed, the PSD program has, in effect, set varying ambient standards, for example, for scenically valuable areas like national parks.

However, there is a "specific egalitarian" justification for the current policy—that of guaranteeing all citizens some minimum level of healthful air. But even if that rationale is accepted, there remains the question of what level should be chosen. The large ad hoc margins of safety that have been invoked to justify some current standards, and the notion that even the most sensitive individual should be protected, are receiving much criticism. Such pressures on the standards are only likely to increase in an expanded marketable rights regime. This may be appropriate in the sense that it will focus political energy and attention on what, in fact, is the relevant parameter. But I believe we must make the conceptual basis for choosing ambient levels more explicit and sophisticated if it is to withstand the increased attention it is already beginning to receive.

Under current law, it would appear that the EPA administrator is precluded from taking economic costs into account in setting an air quality standard. Instead, his task is to protect the public health. However, if the population damage function is like the one in Figure 6–1, there is no safe level for the administrator to pick that totally protects the most sensitive individual in the population. Hence, even today, a balance between costs and benefits is in fact being struck, if only implicitly in the way terms like "health-effect" and "sensitive individual" are used in practice. Environmentalists oppose changing the language of the statute to call for explicit balancing on the grounds that so doing will lead to inappropriately weak standards, partially because polluters will be better able than anyone else to influence the standard-setting process. My own view is that in a democratic society, successful long-run defense of environmental values requires convincing the mass of the public that the gains from such efforts are worth the costs. And from that perspective, explicit decisions and open discussions are sufficiently desirable to make statutory change appropriate.

Finally, it is worth asking whether or not the idea of allowing regulatees to make cost-reducing counter-proposals might not have more general applicability beyond air pollution control. Admittedly, other examples are not easy to find. Occasionally, airlines with an obligation to serve certain communities under the terms of their Civil Aeronautics Board licenses have paid smaller commuter airlines to provide the service for them, which the latter could do more cheaply given its different equipment, mode of operation, and so forth. Some analysts have proposed the use of marketable licenses as a way of restricting chlorofluorocarbon production, and economists have long advocated auctions as a way of allocating the electromagnetic spectrum. In some of these instances, distributional concerns could well limit our willingness to use markets. For example, I doubt that we would be willing to let one coal mine be more dangerous than the rules permit if it pays another mine to be safer than required. Nonetheless, with appropriately modest expectations and a willingness to both accept and seek out the most cost-reducing compromises, I believe further uses for the artificial markets technique could usefully be developed.

NOTES

1. See, for example, Kneese and Schultze (1975), Friedlander (1978), and Dorfman and Dorfman (1977). The last source reprints many of the classic papers in this discussion.

2. The initial statement of the tradeoff policy was in the so-called Interpretive Ruling issued in December of 1976 (see *Federal Regulations* 41: 55525, 55528). This has since been modified by the 1977 Clean Air Act Amendment, Sections 171 to 178. The bubble policy has gone through a number of transformations. The last move of the previous administration is summarized in an EPA press release, January 16, 1981, "Detailed Statement on Bubble Policy Changes." For a more accessible summary see *Environment Reporter* (1981).

3. Do note, however, that Pigou (1932:194) was conscious of the limits of this scheme: ". . . when the interrelations of the various private

persona affected are highly complex, the Government may find it
necessary to exercise some means of administrative control in addition to providing a bounty.''

4. One of the earliest statements of his views is found in Kneese (1964).
5. The argument has been made explicitly since the 1930s. See, for ex-
    ample, the well-known paper by Bergson (1938).
6. In addition to the papers cited in note 1 *supra,* see also Buchanan
    (1968).
7. Introduced by Senator Proxmire, the bill would have set a nationally
    uniform fee on SO_2 emissions.
8. Their proposals are discussed in Selig (1971).
9. At one point a proposal was made in Wisconsin to sell discharge per-
    mits that would permit varying discharges as a function of stream
    flow and stream temperature.
10. See note 2 *supra.*
11. The 1977 Amendments made the tradeoff policy one of several op-
    tions a state may choose among in designing its SIP.
12. This statistic is based on conversations with EPA and EPA contractor
    personnel.
13. A classic discussion of the water law issues can be found in Hirsh-
    leifer et al. (1960).
14. In the closing days of the previous administration, a complex set of
    ''banking'' regulations that would have permitted extensive banking
    was progressing through the internal approval process. As of this
    writing, they have not yet been issued.
15. LAER was intended to be even more restrictive than emissions al-
    lowed under the act for new sources generally, the so-called NSPS, or
    New Source Performance Standards.
16. This finding is based on conversations with EPA personnel.
17. See note 2 *supra.*

REFERENCES

Bator, Francis M. 1958. "The Anatomy of Market Failure," *Quarterly
    Journal of Economics* 72 (August): 351–79.
Bergson, Abram. 1938. "A Reformulation of Certain Aspects of Welfare
    Economics." *Quarterly Journal of Economics* 52 (February): 310–34.
Buchanan, James M. 1968. *The Demand and Supply of Public Goods.*
    Chicago: Rand McNally and Company.
Dales, J.H. 1968. *Pollution, Property and Prices.* Toronto: University of
    Toronto Press.
Dorfman, Robert, and Nancy Dorfman, eds. 1977. *Economics of the En-
    vironment: Selected Readings,* 2d ed. New York: W.W. Norton.

Environmental Protection Agency. 1980. "Emission Density Zoning Manual." Research Triangle Park: Office of Air Quality Programs and Standards.

Environment Reporter 2, no. 29: 1761–62, January 23, 1981.

Friedlander, Ann, ed. 1978. *Approaches to Controlling Air Pollution.* Cambridge, Mass.: MIT Press.

Goklany, I. 1980. "An Investigation of Prevention of Significant Deterioration of Air Quality and Emission Offset Permitting Processes." Washington, D.C.: National Commission on Air Quality.

Hirshleifer, Jack et al. 1960. *Water Supply.* Chicago: University of Chicago Press.

Jacoby, H., and G. Schaumberg. 1965. "Administered Markets in Quality Control: A Proposal for the Delaware Estuary." Unpublished paper, Harvard University.

Kneese, Allen V. 1964. *The Economics of Regional Water Quality Management.* Baltimore: Johns Hopkins Press.

Kneese, Allen V., and Charles L. Schultze. 1975. *Pollution, Prices and Public Policy.* Washington, D.C.: Brookings Institution.

Mishan, E.J. 1969. *Technology and Growth: The Price We Pay.* New York: Praeger.

Montgomery, W.D. 1972. "Markets in Licenses and Efficient Pollution Control Programs." *Journal of Economic Theory* 5, no. 4 (December): 395–418.

Pigou, A.C. 1932. *The Economics of Welfare,* 4th ed., Part II, Chapter 9, Section B, p. 194. London: Macmillan.

Roberts, M.J. 1972. "Alternative Criteria for Social Choice: A Normative Approach." Discussion Paper No. 264. Cambridge: Harvard Institute of Economic Research (December).

Roberts, M.J. 1975. "Environmental Protection: The Complexities of Real Policy Choice." In *Managing the Water Environment,* edited by I.M. Fox and N. Swainson. Vancouver: University of British Columbia Press.

Roberts, M.J. 1980. "The Political Economy of the Clean Water Act of 1972: Why No One Listened to the Economists." In *The Utilization of the Social Sciences in Policy Making in the United States.* Paris: O.E.C.D.

Roberts, M.J., and M. Spence. 1976. "Effluent Charges and Licenses under Uncertainty." *Journal of Public Ecnomics* 5, no. 3: 193–208.

Roberts, M.J., and R.B. Stewart. 1976. "Energy and the Environment." In *Setting National Priorities: The Next Ten Years,* edited by H. Owen and C. Schultze, pp. 411–56. Washington, D.C.: Brookings Institution.

Selig, E.I. 1971. *Effluent Charges on Air and Water Pollution: A Conference Report.* Washington, D.C.: Council on Law Related Studies, Environmental Law Institute.

Thomas, S. 1980. "Politics and Markets." Ph.D. dissertation, Harvard University.

Weitzman, Martin L. 1974. "Prices versus Quantities." *Review of Economic Studies* 41, no. 4 (October): 391–403.

7 DESIGNING A MARKET FOR TRADABLE EMISSIONS PERMITS

Robert W. Hahn and Roger G. Noll

Since the late 1970s, environmental regulators have begun to give serious attention to alternatives to source-specific technical standards as a means for controlling pollution. Indeed, a limited, highly constrained form of one such alternative—tradable emissions permits—began to be implemented for a few air pollutants in some regions. Less constrained methods for implementing tradable permits are actively under consideration. Notable examples include the proposals being considered by the Environmental Protection Agency (EPA) for controlling chlorofluorocarbons and by the California Air Resources Board for reducing particulate sulfates in the Los Angeles airshed.

The purpose of this chapter is to investigate the practicality of a system of tradable emissions permits. The central issue is not whether a market for emissions permits will work perfectly, but whether it can produce a more efficient combination of emissions and abatement strategies than the traditional regulatory approach. This question is examined in the context of a particular pollutant in a specific area, namely, the control of sulfur oxides (SO_x) emissions into the atmosphere in Los Angeles. Nevertheless, we believe the analysis to be of general interest. It raises questions that must be answered in order

The work reported here was supported by the California Air Resources Board. Glen Cass provided useful comments on an earlier draft, and Richard Hanson provided data management support. We are solely responsible for the contents of this chapter.

to make a tradable permits system a practical alternative anywhere. It also illustrates the range of institutional arrangements and informational requirements that must be considered in developing a market for permits.

The tradable permits system examined here is a more radical institutional change than has previously been adopted by regulatory authorities. The "controlled trading options" developed by EPA since the passage of the Clean Air Act amendments of 1977—so-called bubbles, offsets, and emissions banks—start with the existing regulatory structure as a baseline, and overlay it with the possibility of trades.[1] These trading options retain detailed regulatory reviews of each source and of proposed trades. Moreover, traded permits have a somewhat clouded, secondary legal status in comparison to untraded permits.

The approach examined here replaces, rather than supplements, the regulatory methods that are now used to control emissions at their source. It would eliminate distinctions among sources on the basis of age, ownership, industry, or method of acquiring permits. It would simply establish a ceiling on total emissions within a geographic area, and it would allow the allocation of emissions among sources in the area to be determined solely by the market. No regulatory approval of the methods used by any source nor of the distribution of emissions permits among the sources would be required. Policy issues relating to the differential air quality effects of different geographical distributions of emissions permits would be dealt with by the way in which trading regions were defined, and by the rules for trading across regional boundaries. The role of the government would be reduced to the following activities: (1) establishing ambient air quality standards; (2) determining the total amount of emissions in a geographic area that is consistent with the air quality standard; (3) issuing permits and organizing a market for them; and (4) enforcing the emissions limits by ascertaining whether each source is emitting pollutants at or below the rate allowed by the quantity of permits it holds, and by imposing noncompliance penalties. (Regulators also may wish to use direct regulation, rather than a tradable permits system, to deal with air pollution "episodes" that arise when meteorological conditions are unfavorable. See Hahn and Noll (1982) for a more complete discussion of this problem.)

The scholarly literature[2] has examined in detail the theoretical advantages and problems of a system of tradable emissions permits. A competitive market in enforceable emissions permits will achieve a given emissions target at minimum cost and will provide more effective incentives to pursue cost-reducing innovations in abatement technology than does the standards approach—advantages that are also characteristic of emissions taxes. In addition, tradable permits have possible political advantages in comparison to emissions taxes in that they do not necessarily require that the government collect revenues for allowable emissions (the permits can be given away), and they cause the uncertainties associated with environmental policy to be focused more on the total costs of the policy and less on the equilibrium quantity of emissions. Finally, in comparison with current approaches to environmental regulation, a competitive permits market provides fewer barriers to entry for new or expanded pollution sources, and imposes less demanding requirements on regulators.

A major question concerning the practicality of tradable emissions permits is whether a competitive market can be established. Ideally, a market in permits would have a large number of buyers and sellers who actively trade permits, quickly establish a market price for permits that is close to the long-run equilibrium, and take actions that minimize abatement costs and distribute emissions geographically and temporally such that ambient air quality standards are met. In practice, this ideal may not be feasible.

One potential problem is the structure of the permits market. One or a few sources of pollution might account for such a high proportion of emissions that the permits market will be imperfectly competitive, leading to strategic market behavior by the major polluters that prevents the market from allocating permits in a manner that minimizes total abatement costs. Even if the market is not concentrated, the number of participants may be too few to produce more than very infrequent transactions. This, in turn, could lead to costly bilateral negotiations for effecting trades. Moreover, infrequent trades would produce infrequent and possibly highly variable price signals that undermine the ability of polluters to make efficient choices of levels and methods of abatement. These problems have already arisen in attempts to implement EPA's offset and banking policies.

Another potential problem arises from the geographic specificity of both emissions and damages from pollution. Each receptor is polluted by a somewhat different combination of sources, the emissions from which interact—sometimes nonlinearly—to produce unique effects. To guarantee maximum technical efficiency (ignoring the costs of operating the markets) requires that a separate market be established for pollution at each receptor point. Each firm would have to know the relationship between its emissions and pollution at every receptor, and then would have to buy the appropriate amount of pollution permits for each one that it affects. Ignoring this feature of pollution problems and establishing a single permits market for an extensive geographic area could lead to a concentration of emissions from one location that, in turn, would create a localized "hot spot" which is badly out of compliance with ambient pollution standards. Alternatively, creating numerous markets that account for the complexities of the relationship between emissions and pollution could make the costs of organizing and participating in an effective market system so high that it is not worth doing. Moreover, a system with numerous interrelated markets may have some markets in which only one or a few polluters participate, leading to inefficiencies resulting from market concentration.

Whether these potential difficulties offset the theoretical advantages of a system of tradable permits is an empirical question, the answer to which depends upon technical aspects of the pollution problem that is being addressed and the details of the design of the permits market. Both potential problems—imperfect competition and localized pollution hot spots—arise because of a particular perversity in the cost-minimizing distribution of permits. Hence, to determine whether either problem is likely to be a serious drawback to a specific system of marketable permits requires analyzing the likely operation of the market to see if the hypothetical competitive equilibrium distribution of permits is vulnerable to these perversities. To undertake such an analysis requires two types of information: the abatement cost functions faced by each important source of emissions in the region in question, and a model of the relationship between emissions and pollution that has sufficient geographical resolution that it can predict the effects of alternative patterns of emissions on the pattern of pollution within the area.

The abatement cost functions provide the information necessary to determine the distribution of emissions permits for a specific market system. A pollution source that is operated in an economically rational way will minimize the sum of expenditures on permits and on abatement measures for any given level of operation. Higher permit prices generally will lead to fewer purchases of permits and greater abatement. Hence, knowledge of the abatement cost function for each source provides the information necessary to calculate the demand curve for permits for each source and, by addition, for the entire market. These demand relationships can then be used to estimate the market's allocation of permits among sources for any given total quantity of permits. This is accomplished by using the market demand curve to find the equilibrium price of the given quantity of permits, and then using each source-specific demand curve to estimate the equilibrium distribution of permits. The model of the relationship between emissions and pollution can then be used to predict the distribution of pollution that the market would produce.

Alternative designs of a system of tradable permits can be compared by simulating the operation of each. For example, the definition of the geographic scope of a market—which sources are required to buy which permits—is a design variable that can be used to find the best tradeoff between problems of market structure and problems arising from pollution hot spots. As the geographic area in which permits can be freely traded grows more extensive, more sources are incorporated into the market and hence problems of market concentration and infrequent transactions are diminished; however, the likelihood of localized pollution hot spots is increased.

IS IMPLEMENTATION FEASIBLE?

To investigate the viability of marketable permits without actually implementing the alternative requires selecting a specific pollutant, identifying the key implementation problems, and then determining whether a well-designed market will successfully address these issues. As an example, the problem of controlling particulate sulfates in the Los Angeles region was selected. This problem was chosen because its technical characteristics make it a likely candidate for marketable permits, as is discussed below.

The current approach toward controlling sulfur oxides emissions in Los Angeles relies on source-specific standards, an offset policy, and a modest emissions fee. Large new sources of pollution must adopt the best available technology, and must trade off the uncontrolled portion of their emissions by effecting further reductions at existing sources in the Los Angeles Basin. The owner of an existing source is thus vested with a valuable property right which can be sold in whole or in part to new sources. The owner also has the option of retaining the opportunity for further abatement to facilitate subsequent expansion.

As discussed above, the offset policy is one limited form of a market in transferable permits to emit air pollutants. Its principal drawbacks are that the costs of negotiation are excessive, the number of trades that can be made by new sources is limited, all trades must be approved by several regulatory authorities before they can be consummated, and, in any case, sources must satisfy minimum technical standards before and after trades. Negotiation costs are high because new entrants must first identify existing sources of pollution where emissions reductions are feasible, and then try to estimate a reasonable charge for the offset. Moreover, gains from trade are limited to the extent that existing technical standards do not allow marginal abatement costs to be equated across firms.

The question at hand is whether a market for SO_x emissions permits could improve matters. First, the criteria for measuring the success of a market proposal need to be specified. For this specific case a market should satisfy established air quality goals for sulfate particulates in a more cost-effective manner than the current system of source-specific standards, should encourage investment in finding more cost-effective abatement technologies for the future, and should be legally and politically feasible. Legal feasibility means that the market must meet the requirements of relevant constitutional constraints, and be implementable without fundamental changes in the performance objectives of existing statutes. Political feasibility means that the regulatory agency should be capable of administering the program; furthermore, some degree of support from industry, the public, and regulators is needed if the approach is to stand a chance of being adopted.

To demonstrate feasibility requires a good technical understanding of the problem. The particulate sulfate problem in Los Angeles is caused primarily by the combustion of sulfur-bearing energy sources. Particulate sulfates are a regulatory concern because they reduce visibility, acidify rainwater, and may have harmful health effects. The conversion of SO_x emissions to sulfates in Los Angeles can be thought of as proceeding in three stages. First, sulfur enters the air basin. Virtually all of the sulfur that is emitted in Los Angeles is initially embodied in crude oil. Second, when oil products are refined or burned without controls, some of the sulfur they contain is converted to SO_2

and SO_3 and released to the atmosphere. Finally, the SO_x compounds react to form sulfates through a series of atmospheric chemical processes.

Cass (1978) has succeeded in constructing an emissions/air quality model for particulate sulfates in Los Angeles. He has shown that the relation between SO_x emissions and sulfate air quality in Los Angeles is approximately linear and, in addition, can be modeled adequately as if it were largely independent of the level of other key pollutants. One feature of Cass's model is that mobile sources are treated as stationary sources by converting them to traffic densities over the airshed. Because the most efficient strategy for reducing sulfur emissions from mobile sources is to reduce the sulfur content of fuels, regulation of mobile sources can be done indirectly by placing the responsibility on refiners. A tradable permits system could then require refiners to add refinery emissions to SO_x emissions from mobile sources to determine the number of permits they must hold.

A major task of the project was to estimate abatement cost functions for the primary sources of sulfur oxides emissions in Los Angeles. Over twenty-five source categories were identified, and abatement costs estimated for each. The published literature, regulatory proceedings, and interviews with representatives of local industry and state and local regulatory personnel were relied upon to generate preliminary cost estimates. The information typically obtained from a particular source was a point estimate—the cost at some historical date of using a particular method to obtain a specific rate of emissions from a particular kind of facility. These were combined to produce a step function for abatement costs for representative facilities in each source category based on 1977 regulatory conditions, with corrections made to put the costs in 1977 dollars. The results of these analyses were submitted as industry studies to the relevant firms operating in Los Angeles, with requests for comments. The additional data received in this manner were used to produce a final cost study, including indications of the amount of disagreement about costs among the sources of information.

A number of factors make these cost estimates upwardly biased as estimators of the costs that would be experienced if a system of tradable permits were instituted. First, for source categories for which no control cost estimates could be found, emissions were assumed to be uncontrollable. Second, production and energy use at emitting facilities were assumed to be independent of the amount of control. In reality, firms with especially high emissions and stiff abatement costs are likely to reduce output or to make more efficient use of energy. Third, although in many cases emissions can be reduced by process changes, firms are reluctant to reveal these possibilities because they are trade secrets that may confer significant competitive advantages in a more stringent regulatory environment. No allowance for these process changes is made in the study.

Because SO_x emissions in Los Angeles result largely from the combustion of petroleum products, the availability of natural gas, which has negligible amounts of sulfur, can significantly affect SO_x emissions. This, in turn, will affect the demand for permits and, hence, their price. Price regulation has led to excess demand for natural gas since the mid-1960s, and to uncertainties about the availability of gas in the future, even though gas is now scheduled to be deregulated. For this reason, three separate cases were analyzed: one which assumes low availability of natural gas, a second which corresponds to a historical supply year (1973) in which an intermediate supply of gas was available, and a third which assumes a high supply of natural gas. All three cases are based on emissions projections for the early 1980s with 1977 regulations assumed to be in place. In all cases, access to natural gas is assumed to be determined by regulatory allocation priorities rather than the market. This has an important effect on the results because regulatory allocation priorities are not related to the value of natural gas in terms of either its direct use or the effects of its use on air quality.

With these caveats in mind, the cost data were used to estimate the demand for emissions permits and the distribution of permits that an efficient market would produce.

THE COMPETITIVE MODEL

In all of the models discussed, it is assumed that firms attempt to minimize the sum of abatement costs plus permit costs. In this section, a baseline competitive equilibrium distribution of emissions permits is simulated. Firms are assumed to be price-takers, which is to say they assume that the equilibrium price of a permit is unaffected by their actions. A permit is defined as the right to emit one ton SO_2 equivalent of SO_x per day anywhere in the airshed. After examining this baseline case, it will be compared to a fine-tuned definition of permits that takes account of the geographical locations of sources and receptors, and to a simulated distribution of emissions when the permits are monopsonized.

To simulate the market, it is necessary to specify an air quality target. For the purposes of analysis, four targets are examined, ranging from no further net emissions control to about a 70 percent reduction in emissions. The latter is needed to meet the California sulfate standard. The four cases are summarized in Table 7-1.

The calculations in the table are based on a linear rollback model of the relationship between emissions and sulfate pollution. The estimates of the emissions/air quality relationship would probably change if a more sophisticated air pollution model were employed, but the rollback model suffices for the purpose of showing how the permit price and abatement costs vary with the choice of an air quality target. Figure 7-1 illustrates the equilibrium price of a permit to emit one ton per day of SO_x in Los Angeles for the case in which there is a low natural gas supply. All price and cost estimates are given in 1977 dollars.

The decreasing step function in Figure 7-1 represents the derived demand curve for permits over the range of interest. The curve was drawn as a step function because most of the engineering cost estimates which were used to generate the demand curves were given in

Table 7-1. Selected Air Quality Targets for the South Coast Air Basin (tons SO_x/day).[a]

Target	Allowable Emissions
1. Achieve California Sulfate Air Quality Standard of 25 micrograms/cubic meter over a 24 hour averaging time.	149
2. Violate California Sulfate Air Quality Standard 3-5% of the time.	238
3. No additional controls with an above average natural gas supply.	335
4. No additional controls with a low natural gas supply.	421

[a]See Hahn (1981b) for the basis of these calculations. Sulfur oxides emissions are measured as tons of SO_2 equivalent.

Figure 7-1. The Demand for Permits with Low Availability of Natural Gas.

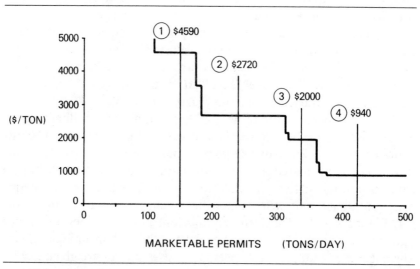

MARKETABLE PERMITS   (TONS/DAY)

Source: Hahn (1981a).

this form. The four vertical supply constraints in Figure 7-1 correspond to the four air quality targets presented in Table 7-1. The market price of a permit is drawn next to each intersection. Thus for the first case in which the California sulfate standard is met, the point estimate for the price of a permit is $4,590. Based on the derived demand for permits, it is also possible to calculate two other potentially interesting numbers. The amount of money which could conceivably change hands in a permit market can be calculated by multiplying the number of permits issued by the equilibrium price. The annual abatement cost for any level of air quality can be computed by integrating the area under the entire demand curve and to the right of the air quality target, and then multiplying by 365. (Because Figure 7-1 only shows the main part of the curve, and not the curve in its entirety, it is not possible to reconstruct abatement cost numbers from the figure.) The significance of these numbers is discussed below.

The price of an emissions permit is highly sensitive to the availability of natural gas and to the choice of an air quality target. Table 7-2 shows the equilibrium price of a permit with alternative assumptions about air quality standards and the availability of natural gas. Table 7-2 exhibits two interesting features. First, it can be seen that

Table 7-2. Permit Price Sensitivity Analysis.

Natural Gas Supply	Air Quality Target			
	1	*2*	*3*	*4*
Low	4,590[a]	2,720	2,000	940
Historical	2,720	2,000	940	810
High	1,320	650	470	420

[a]All prices in 1977 dollars. A permit entitles the user to emit one ton of SO_x for one day.
Source: Hahn (1981a).

the price of a permit can vary by an order of magnitude depending on the assumptions concerning natural gas supply and the air quality target. Second, a comparison of the first two columns indicates that a fairly small change in air quality standards causes a substantial change in the price of a permit. This reflects the fact that the marginal cost of SO_x abatement increases more rapidly at the upper end of the air quality spectrum.

The total annual cost of abatement varies considerably both as a function of the natural gas supply and the air quality target. The data are presented in Table 7-3. The estimates of abatement cost do *not* include abatement equipment installed prior to 1977. Consequently, the changes in abatement cost between different categories are probably the most meaningful figures. Even without estimates of some abatement equipment in place, abatement costs are in the hundreds of millions, except for the case in which natural gas is in plentiful supply.

Table 7-3. Annual Abatement Costs (millions of 1977 dollars).

Natural Gas Supply	Air Quality Target			
	1	*2*	*3*	*4*
Low	684	576	487	447
Historical	400	315	280	252
High	112	83	66	53

Source: Hahn (1981a).

The most important point to be derived from Table 7–3 is that the availability of natural gas has a marked effect on the cost of reducing SO_x emissions. The only difference between the situations of low and high natural gas supply is that the latter substitutes natural gas for 100 million barrels of residual fuel oil. Dividing the difference in abatement costs between the two cases by the difference in the amount of oil used yields an average cost saving per barrel-equivalent of natural gas between $4 and $6, depending on the air quality target. The cost savings result from the substitution of natural gas for high-sulfur fuel oil, rather than using low-sulfur oil or extensive abatement investments to meet emissions targets.

Another way of illustrating the critical importance of the natural gas supply is to ask what firms would be willing to pay for having natural gas substituted for one barrel of residual fuel oil. Assume that the marginal value of natural gas equals the full marginal cost of burning residual fuel oil. The full cost includes the price of a barrel of oil plus the cost of emitting or abating the associated SO_x. Performing the calculation for all twelve cases reveals that firms would be willing to pay anywhere from 107 percent to 130 percent of the price of the residual fuel oil for an equivalent British thermal unit (Btu) amount of natural gas.

In evaluating the desirability of a system of marketable permits, one important issue is the potential savings in the costs of regulation. Of course, most of the opportunities for cost savings are not easily quantified. For example, a system of tradable emission permits will tend to produce lower barriers to entry than the current emission standards approach; however, placing a meaningful dollar estimate on the expected net benefits from such a change is difficult. It is also difficult to know to what extent the marketable permit system will induce innovations in abatement technology over time. Finally, the costs of the regulatory process should be lower under tradable permits, but the magnitude of the savings is uncertain. The following analysis focuses solely on the static efficiency gains which can accrue from using a market mechanism. Moreover, attention will be restricted to that subset of static gains not involving process changes, which could be substantial for industries such as petroleum refiners. Thus, the estimates developed here are best viewed as a lower bound on the actual gains that might result from moving to marketable permits.

For SO_x emissions in Los Angeles, the gains from using an incentive-based approach to maintain the status quo can be expected to be relatively small in comparison to other applications which have been examined. This is because the local pollution control agency has attempted to use cost-effectiveness as a major criterion in promulgating rules.

The specific problem is to examine how the competitive equilibrium under a tradable emissions permit system compares with the current standards approach to regulation. The first step in the analysis is to project the level of expected emissions under standards. This calculation is performed for all three levels of natural gas supply and two sets of standards. The first set of standards consists of those in place by the end of 1977. The second set consists of those expected to be in place by 1985. The projected emissions for the six cases are shown in Table 7-4. Note that the projected emissions for the low natural gas scenario under 1977 standards correspond to case 4 in Table 7-1. The predicted emissions in 1985 are lower than 1977 SO_x emissions because the former standards include more stringent controls on three source categories: petroleum coke calciners, fluid catalytic crackers and residual fuel burning by refiners.

The next step in the analysis is to compare the cost of standards with the competitive equilibrium for an emissions permit market. The difference is the expected annual savings in moving from standards to tradable emissions permits, which is shown in Table 7-5. The data show that some cost savings are possible, even though regulators have tried to implement cost-effective control strategies.

The last point which the anlaysis of the competitive case raises is the magnitude of the sums of money which could conceivably change hands if a market were to be implemented in a way that caused all permits to be sold, such as a public auction. Define the total annualized value of the permits as the number issued multiplied by the annual price people are willing to pay to hold a permit for one year. (This price is obtained by multiplying the data in Table 7-2 by 365.)

Table 7-4. Sulfur Oxides Emissions under Standards (tons SO_x/day).

	Standards	
Natural Gas	1977	1985
Low	421	364
Historical	298	250
High	211	167

Source: Hahn (1981a).

Table 7–5. Annual Cost Savings with an Undifferentiated Tradable Permit System (millions of 1977 dollars).

	Standards	
Natural Gas	1977	1985
Low	23	22
Historical	17	15
High	10	8

Source: Hahn (1981a).

For the twelve cases examined here, the total annual value of the permits varies between 65 and 250 million dollars, and is generally only slightly smaller than the corresponding annualized abatement costs. This may have considerable political significance. The initial allocation of permits, establishing the baseline from which trades are made, is an implicit allocation of a considerable amount of wealth—indeed, the magnitude of the wealth inherent in the permits is likely to be large in comparison to the efficiency gains from a permits market. Consequently, the principal focus of the political debate over alternative market designs is likely to be wealth distribution, not efficiency.

DOES FINE-TUNING PAY?

The preceding analysis deals with the case in which emissions permits are freely tradable throughout the airshed, with no account taken of the differences among sources in the impact of emissions on ambient air quality. Instead of having a single market where permits are undifferentiated, imagine a case where there are several markets corresponding to each of the receptors within an air quality region. Assume further that firms would have to participate in all markets where their individual emissions affect air quality. This is the essence of the fine-tuning problem. In practice, a fine-tuned permits market would be difficult to implement; however, the outcome of such a system, assuming it could be implemented, can be simulated in the same fashion as the case of a competitive market for geographically unspecified permits.

The results of the simulations for this case are shown in Table 7-6. Column (1) lists six alternative levels of total emissions to be allowed in the airshed. Column (2) shows the abatement costs for achieving these levels, assuming a competitive permits market and low availability of natural gas. The low natural gas case was selected because it generates the highest abatement costs and, therefore, is likely to produce the maximal benefits from fine-tuning.

Associated with the competitive distribution of each of the emissions levels in Column (1) is a set of the average concentrations of sulfate particulates during the year at each of the seventeen air quality monitoring sites used in the simulation. Suppose that instead of setting a limit on total emissions, regulators issue permits to pollute at each receptor point equal to the pollution that would result from the competitive equilibrium in the emissions permit market. Each source of emissions would then need to acquire separately permits for the pollution its emissions caused at every measuring station. Because geographical location matters in affecting measured air pollution, this approach could produce additional rearrangements of emissions—and some increase in total emissions—that result in lower abatement costs but do not reduce air quality at any measuring station. Column (3) shows the costs associated with the competitive equilibrium distribution of emissions under this system.

Table 7-6. Annual Abatement Costs and Market Arrangements (millions of 1977 dollars).

(1) Baseline Emissions Target (tons/day SO_2 equiv)	(2) Costs for Single Market in Emissions Permits	(3) Costs for Equivalent Multiple Air Quality Markets	(4) Costs for "Adjusted" Multiple Air Quality Markets
150	682	682	682
200	614	606	594
250	565	557	545
300	515	513	505
350	476	473	464
400	455	448	436

Note: Assumes "low" natural gas availability.
Source: Hahn (1981a).

Finally, suppose regulators are concerned only with air quality at the worst measuring station, and that they create permits for each station that allow pollution at every monitoring station to equal the pollution measured at the worst station under the competitive equilibrium distribution of emissions permits in Column (1). This would allow further trades and increases in emissions as long as air quality did not deteriorate at the location with the worst pollution, and did not force some other station to have its air quality deteriorate beyond the level at the worst-case station. The abatement costs associated with the competitive equilibrium distribution of these permits is shown in Column (4).

The result of these simulations is that defining permits in terms of pollution, and geographically differentiating the permits for each monitoring location, has relatively little effect on the efficiency of the market. The differences in annual abatement costs under the three systems vary from zero to four percent of the total, amounts that are surely small compared to the difficulties of trying to implement a more complicated system.

There are two qualifications to the basic result that a finely tuned system may not be warranted on the basis of cost savings. First, it should be noted that air quality is measured in terms of average annual concentrations. A shorter averaging time could produce a different result. Second, the result speaks to the present. Calculations are based upon the abatement possibilities and emissions inventories of existing firms in their current locations. Changes in the economic structure of the airshed conceivably could alter the pattern of emissions such that a more complicated system would provide substantial benefits. But, at present, there does not appear to be a serious loss in efficiency associated with adopting the simplest approach of making emissions permits freely transferable throughout the airshed.

THE EFFECTS OF MARKET POWER

Thus far the analysis has been restricted to the case in which firms act as price-takers in the permits market. One potential problem with a marketable permits system is that one or a few firms may be able to manipulate the market to their advantage and, in the extreme, destroy its efficiency advantages over standards. This problem cannot be dismissed lightly for the case at hand.

The source producing the highest rate of emissions is an electric utility. Table 7-7 shows the estimated share of total emissions that it would produce under the competitive market allocation, which ranges between one-fourth to one-half of the permits. Whether this will, in fact, allow the firm to exercise significant market power is an open question that depends on how the market is organized and operates. For purposes of analysis, we will assume that this sizable market share allows the firm to exercise market power.

The market power of the firm with the largest market share could manifest itself in several ways. It is not even clear without further specification of the details of the design of the market whether a firm with market power will act as a monopolistic seller of permits or as a monopsonistic buyer.[3] Here we will analyze the case of a monopsonistic buyer. We assume that the firm in question initially will be given fewer permits than it is expected to want to hold after the market in permits is opened. This is consistent with present policies that tend to require utilities to adopt abatement methods having higher marginal abatement cost than is common for most other industries. For the numerical simulation discussed below, we assume that the utility will receive no permits initially, and that it will be the only purchaser of permits—that is, the initial distribution of permits is such that the utility will be able to exercise maximal market power. In such a market, the equilibrium price will equal the marginal abatement cost of the sellers of permits, but not of the monopsonistic buyer. In purchasing permits, the monopsonist will take account of the fact that as it increases its purchases of permits, it will drive up their price. Hence, it will buy fewer permits at a lower price than would be the competitive, cost-minimizing solution. In other words,

Table 7-7. Market Share of the Largest Permit Holder under Competition (percentage).

	Air Quality Target			
Natural Gas Supply	1	2	3	4
Low	31	43	45	41
Historical	32	43	48	48
High	23	29	40	47

Source: Hahn (1981a).

the monopsonist will abate too much in relation to other firms, and the latter will have lower marginal abatement costs than the former. To the monopsonist, some additional, uneconomic abatement will be worthwhile because of its depressing effect on the price paid for the permits that it acquires from other firms.

Table 7-8 shows the simulated market share of the firm holding the most permits, assuming that it achieves the profit-maximizing monopsony. A comparison of Tables 7-7 and 7-8 illustrates the additional abatement that the monopsonist will undertake if it has market power. The two tables also reveal another interesting fact. The market share of the largest firm tends to be high at an intermediate natural gas supply and does not differ much between high and low gas supply. This reflects the fact that at the extremes natural gas is used either sparingly or extensively by almost all industrial sources, while the intermediate case reflects the fact that utilities will be among the last to be allowed to switch to gas from low-sulfur fuel oil under the current scheme for gas allocations.

The decrease in market share is typically accompanied by a decrease in the price of a permit. This can be seen by comparing Table 7-9 with Table 7-2. As in the competitive case, the permit price still varies by an order of magnitude over different assumptions about the air quality target and the supply of natural gas.

Although the differences between the competitive and monopsonistic case appear large, whether they cause a major loss of efficiency in achieving abatement targets remains an open question. The appropriate measure of inefficiency is neither price nor market share, but the differences in total abatement costs under the two situations. If at the competitive equilibrium all firms face a fairly flat marginal abate-

Table 7-8. Market Share of the Largest Permit Holder under Market Power (percentage).

Natural Gas Supply	Air Quality Target			
	1	2	3	4
Low	20	31	37	41
Historical	32	40	33	44
High	23	25	39	32

Source: Hahn (1981a).

Table 7-9. Permit Prices under Market Power.

Natural Gas Supply	Air Quality Target			
	1	2	3	4
Low	2,720[a]	2,000	1,000	940
Historical	2,720	1,000	650	470
High	1,000	470	420	210

[a]All prices are in 1977 dollars. A permit entitles the user to emit one ton of SO_x per day.
Source: Hahn (1981a).

ment cost over a wide range of emissions reductions, a large shift of emissions from the monopsonist to the rest of the firms might entail relatively little loss of efficiency. As can be seen in Figure 7-1, all of the choices of alternative ambient air quality standards happen to fall within relatively flat portions of the demand curve for permits, and therefore in areas in which the abatement cost function obeys essentially constant marginal costs. Calculations of the efficiency loss of market power were made in each case, and the loss was determined to be relatively small, ranging from zero to ten percent depending upon the particular combination of assumptions about natural gas supplies, ambient air quality standards, and the method used for estimating the abatement cost functions.

Nevertheless, a conclusion that market power will not severely undermine the operation of the market is not warranted at this time. The estimated loss in efficiency due to market power is quite sensitive to small changes in the cost functions. Consequently, considerable thought must be given to the possibility of building protections against monopsonistic market power into the tradable permits system. These issues are addressed in the following section, which focuses on questions of institutional design.

INITIALIZING THE MARKET

The major design criteria for a tradable emissions permit market are: equity in the initial distribution of permits; sufficient early transactions to produce a stable price for permits that is close enough to the long-run equilibrium to encourage rational long-term investment planning; and attainment of an equilibrium price and distribution of permits that is close enough to the competitive case to assure attainment of air quality objectives at lower costs than can be obtained by alternative regulatory approaches. A major design feature that affects the extent to which a permits market satisfies these criteria is the method for starting up the market.

One way of starting the market is to make an initial allocation of permits, and then to rely on the inefficiencies of this allocation to generate incentives for a market to form. Three methods for initially distributing the permits are considered. One would base the permit distribution on emissions as they existed prior to recent attempts to control them, with perhaps some additional provision for firms that have entered the airshed or expanded capacity since that time. The second would base the initial allocation on the emissions allowed under current standards. The third would base the distribution of permits on the projected equilibrium that would result from a competitive, perfectly efficient market in permits. Any other method that is based upon historical emissions performance raises the objection that people who were early to comply with regulation would be punished for cooperating. Any method that is not based on emissions raises the objection that it is arbitrary, and in any case is more vulnerable to becoming bogged down in a contest between competing claims for redistributing wealth that have nothing to do with air pollution policy.

Basing the initial distribution on the projected competitive equilibrium has a serious defect in terms of efficiency of the permits market. To the extent that the initial distribution succeeded in finding the competitive equilibrium, it would also succeed in avoiding the necessity for any transactions among present sources. Only in the case of new sources or expansions of existing facilities would a demand for trades arise. Thus, a relatively speedy attainment of a stable, competitive price for permits would be least likely under this mechanism. Indeed, much the same problems as confront the current banking and offset policies could be expected: a slow development of the market owing to the difficulties of finding trading partners and negotiating a price.

A second difficulty with the strategy of distributing the permits on the basis of the estimated competitive equilibrium is that it may be more vulnerable to legal challenges and delays. The method for simulating the competitive equilibrium is to minimize estimated abatement costs for the entire airshed—a calculation that is based on numerous estimates of costs for each category of sources at all feasible levels of abatement. This is tantamount to setting new source-specific standards for the entire region. Because the cost estimates on which the equilibrium allocation would be based are admittedly inexact, they are vulnerable to challenge as being insufficiently precise to support a regulatory decision, just as existing source-specific standards are often challenged—and changed or delayed—on the basis of their estimated costs and effectiveness. If any single estimate of abatement costs or efficiency that was used in simulating the competitive equilibrium were successfully challenged, it would undermine the entire initial allocation of permits, and, hence, the implementation of the system.

Other possible candidates for permit distribution are to base initial allocations on an historical level of emissions or current standards. One possibility of the former is the emissions inventory of 1973, while an estimate of the latter is a projection of the 1980 inventory. Both are shown in Table 7-10. These, too, have unfortunate properties. They appear to stack the deck in favor of monopsonistic behavior

Table 7-10. Past and Projected "Market Shares" of Sulfur Oxides Emissions by Source Type for the South Coast Air Basin of California.[a]

	1973 Emissions	1980 Projection Low Natural Gas Scenario	
Source Type	% of Total Emissions[b]	Source Type	% of Total Emissions
Utility	28	Utility	31
Mobile Sources	16	Mobile Sources	27
Utility	11	Utility	10
Oil Company	8	Oil Company	4
Steel Company	7	Coke Calcining Company	4
Oil Company	3	Oil Company	4
Coke Calcining Company	3	Steel Company	3
Oil Company	3	Oil Company	3
Oil Company	2	Oil Company	2
Oil Company	2	Oil Company	2

[a]These figures are based on the 1974 definition of the South Coast Air Basin which was subsequently revised.

[b]Emissions are rounded to the nearest percent.

Source: Calculations by R. Hahn based on Cass (1978) and data used to compile Cass (1979).

by the firm with the largest share of permits. In 1973 and 1980 this firm accounted for 28 and 31 percent of emissions, respectively, as contrasted with a projection of 44 percent under competition, assuming current regulations and historical natural gas availability. Thus, one would expect the largest firm to be a purchaser of permits—and a very large purchaser if the competitive outcome is to be achieved. In either case, it is plausible that in order to achieve the competitive result, the firm with the largest market share must account for nearly all purchases of permits (nearly everyone else would be a seller), and therefore face powerful incentives to engage in monopsonistic purchasing practices.

The dilemma in organizing the permits market is that there is a seeming inconsistency in getting the single largest source of emissions to engage in transactions so as to get the market started quickly on a course that provides stable price signals to firms making abatement and location decisions, and in preventing the market from being manipulated. Several possibilities emerge for attacking this problem.

One approach is to use different methods for the largest emissions source and other sources for making the initial distribution of permits, allocating to the potential monopsonist something like the competitive equilibrium estimate while using the historical basis for allocating permits to others. This would probably produce a situation in which the largest source was not a participant in the early stages of the market; however, the remaining sources would have an incentive to engage in trades, and would be more likely to produce a competitive outcome.

A second approach is to make a distinction between the most important sources as a group and the remaining sources, allocating permits initially so that all of the former are equally interested in acquiring more permits, while all of the latter want to sell. Thus, each of the half-dozen most important sources of emissions could be allocated a number of emissions permits that falls short of the estimated competitive equilibrium by the same absolute amount, while the other firms could be given permits that exceed their estimated equilibrium amount by some proportion that is consistent with the first allocation. In such a situation, the largest source of emissions would hold the largest number of permits, but would not account for an especially large fraction of the transactions on its side of the market.

A third approach is to allocate only some fraction of the permits on the basis of historical or projected emissions, and let the state auction the rest. All firms could, say, be allocated 80 or 90 percent of their projected equilibrium emissions, and the remaining permits would be sold. This has the objection that, like an emissions tax, the state ends up collecting revenues, so that the costs of the system to polluters exceed their abatement costs; however, if the fraction of permits sold were small enough, the efficiency gains to industry in rationalizing abatement control strategies would offset the revenues lost to the auction.

A final possible approach is to use an auction process that redistributes auction revenues to the firms that participate in the market. In order to produce an efficient outcome, the method for determining the rebate to a firm must not depend on its actions in the auction. One possible auction process that generates no net revenue and that has attractive incentive properties is as follows. Each firm would receive a provisional initial allocation, based upon one of the criteria discussed above—historical emissions, current standards, expected competitive equilibrium. All sources would be required to offer their entire allocation for sale. Each firm would then report its demand curve for permits, and the sum of the demand curves would be used to calculate the market-clearing price for the fixed total quantity of permits for the entire market. This price would then be used to calculate the final allocation of permits to each firm, according to its demand curve. Firms would make a gross payment to the state equal to the market price times their final allocation, and would receive a gross revenue from the state equal to the market price times the initial allocation. The net financial effect on each firm would be the market price times the difference between its initial and final allocation; the net financial effect on all firms taken together would be zero.

Initialization methods that use an auction process have two significant advantages over methods that simply define the initial distribution of permits and then wait for normal market forces to cause trades. The first advantage is that all firms are placed on the same side of the market initially—as demanders for state-issued permits. This reduces the likelihood that a large pollution source will be able to exercise market power, for the latter depends on the share of firms' excess demand (or supply) in relation to others on the same side of the market. The second advantage is that all firms participate in the establishment of the auction price, not just the firms that are sufficiently out of equilibrium after the initial allocation of permits that they have a strong enough incentive to orchestrate an early transaction. An auction avoids the transaction costs and other problems of bilateral negotiations for consummating the first exchanges, and maximizes the amount of information conveyed by the initial price signal.

The preceding discussion of these organizational issues has value beyond a particular concern about market power in the context of this case study. While an imperfectly competitive market for permits may not be a common problem, all potential applications of tradable permits involve the selection of an institution for allocating the permits in a manner that satisfies equity constraints and still promotes an efficient market. Whereas the nature of the problems to be overcome in facing a tradeoff between these objectives will differ from case to case, conflicts between efficiency and the political perception of equity are likely to be common. The substantial differences in regulatory standards among industries and between new and old sources are manifestations of the same kinds of conflicts in the current system. Thus, specification of the properties of different methods for distributing permits and organizing trades is an important general issue for making feasible the adoption of tradable permits.

GENERALIZING THE BASIC APPROACH

Even if the formation of a tradable emissions permit market is found to be an attractive policy option for one particular pollutant in a specific locale, the issue still remains as to the generalizability of the result. Will a detailed air quality model always be required for each application? Will new cost estimates need to be developed for each case? In short, will regulators need to undertake an in-depth analysis similar to the one discussed here in order to ascertain whether a market solution is appropriate for a particular problem?

Certainly, some analysis will always be required in thinking about making the transition from "command and control" regulation to a market approach; however, it is likely that as experience with incentive-based options such as markets increases, the level of analysis needed for potential new applications will decrease.

Specifically, what are the critical components with which a regulator should concern himself before considering a market scheme? One is the approximate costs of regulation incurred by the agency and by industry. A second would be the agency's monitoring and enforcement capability. A third important element would be knowledge about the sources of emissions, and a fourth would be an understanding of the relationship between source emissions and measures of environmental quality.

The first point to observe about this list of requirements is that in a general way it is common to the development of a rational environmental policy of any kind. A regulator needs to have some idea of the relationship between emissions and pollution in order to develop a set of standards, tradable emissions permits, or effluent taxes that accomplishes the objectives of environmental policy. Moreover, regulators need to know the preregulation pattern of emissions and the abatement opportunities available to each major source in order to set standards or taxes that will achieve environmental objectives in a cost-effective manner. Finally, all policies must be consistent with the ability of the regulator to monitor emissions and pollution, and to enforce any method of achieving its goal.

Nevertheless, the informational requirements may differ in their details for implementing a system of tradable permits. One reason is that a positive case needs to be made to convince political actors—regulators, regulated businesses, environmentalists, and the public at large—that a change in regulatory methods is worth trying. This is the source of the belief that the initial implementation of a tradable permits system will require a well-documented study of its likely performance, but that subsequent programs will require less information if the initial program succeeds.

Even so, a market approach may require a different combination of analysis and data than other approaches. The reason is that the important regulatory decisions in implementing and maintaining a market system are somewhat different, leading to different evidentiary requirements if a regulatory authority's decisions are to withstand legal and political attacks. A case in point would be the establishment of a baseline emissions inventory upon which to make the initial distribution of permits. Because potentially large implicit wealth transfers are involved, participants in the process to set up a tradable permits system could be expected to take an active interest in establishing a baseline, leading an agency to make a greater commitment of resources to this issue than would otherwise be the case. By the same token, agency expenditures for identifying best control technologies could be reduced, because the agency would no longer need to establish legally defensible source-specific standards. In a world with tradable permits, the key regulatory decisions are the initial allocation of the permits, the establishment of total emissions limits, and the determination of an ambient air quality standard. Regulatory resources would tend to be redirected toward these issues and away from studying problems of specific sources.

As a practical matter, a market approach is likely to retain some standards. In the case reported here, for example, attention was focused entirely on the effect of SO_x emissions on particulate sulfates because the Los Angeles airshed is in compliance with standards for SO_2 concentrations. As discussed above, SO_2 emissions undergo chemical reactions and transportation in the atmosphere to become sulfates. Thus, at any given location, SO_2 pollution is more likely to be the result of a nearby source of SO_2 emissions, whereas particulate sulfates are more likely to be the result of emissions from numerous sources, including some at a relatively great distance. In Los Angeles, compliance with SO_2 standards generally only requires that major emissions sources install tall enough smokestacks so that by the time SO_2 reaches the ground it has been adequately dispersed in the atmosphere to satisfy maximum atmospheric concentrations. The adoption of an emissions market for sulfur in Los Angeles as a means for controlling sulfate pollution would most assuredly be done in the context of a continued requirement of an adequate stack height for major stationary sources of SO_2 emissions. This observation has quite general applicability, for it is commonly the case that a single source of emissions produces several different kinds of pollution: a nearby effect for which it is the only source, and more distant effects that involve interactions with other sources. Markets are well suited for dealing with the latter case, but only within the context of maximum permissible concentrations at the point of emissions in order to avoid exceeding the limits for localized effects. At the extreme, for cases in which localized effects are the binding constraint on emissions for most of the important sources, a tradable permits system could have limited value.

Another situation in which tradable permits may be less attractive is in the case of very complex pollution problems in which several types of emissions interact to form a variety of pollutants, often in nonlinear and even nonmonotonic ways. An example of a complex, nonmonotonic pollution problem is photochemical smog. Smog is the product of chemical reactions involving, among other things, numerous hydrocarbon compounds and oxides of nitrogen (NO_x). For different combinations of emissions in the atmosphere, smog can be either increased or decreased by increasing emissions of NO_x. More generally, the specific kinds and geographic distribution of numerous emissions can be very important in determining the severity of pollution, given a constant level of total emissions for NO_x and hydrocarbons. While this may be successfully attacked by a set of markets for several categories of emissions, perhaps with considerable geographic fine-tuning, it is also possible that a pure market solution will not be practical. Indeed, regulators could well find that they must retain a requirement of prior approval of major transactions of permits for smog components in order to provide the opportunity to investigate their consequences for air quality. Nevertheless, although the problem of determining the feasibility of tradable permits for dealing with smog is far more difficult than the SO_x feasibility problem, the method of this paper is still applicable, with the answer depending on empirical issues relating to the details of the emissions/air quality relationship and the abatement cost functions of emissions sources.

With the preceding caveats in mind, the research to date on the Los Angeles sulfate problem indicates that tradable emissions permits are a promising alternative to command and control regulation. For the case of particulate sulfates in Los Angeles, none of the major sources of market imperfections appear to be so intractable that they cannot be overcome by an intelligently designed market institution. Hence, because of the other beneficial incentive effects of the system, tradable permits for SO_x emissions in Los Angeles appear attractive. Moreover, the analytical issues associated with researching the question of the feasibility of a permits market have also proved to be tractable, suggesting that the same methods might be fruitfully applied to other pollution problems.

NOTES

1. See Hahn and Noll (1982) for a more complete discussion of this issue.
2. Examples include Dales (1968), Montgomery (1972), Roberts and Spence (1976), and Teitenberg (1980).
3. For an analysis of this problem, see Hahn (1981a).

REFERENCES

Cass, G.R. 1978. "Methods for Sulfate Air Quality Management with Applications to Los Angeles." Ph.D. dissertation, Environmental Quality Laboratory, California Institute of Technology, Pasadena.

Cass, G.R. 1979. "Sulfur Oxides Emissions in the Early 1980s under Conditions of Low Natural Gas Supply." Working paper, Environmental Quality Laboratory, California Institute of Technology, Pasadena.

Dales, J.H. 1968. *Pollution, Property and Prices.* Toronto: Toronto University Press.

Hahn, R.W. 1981a. "An Assessment of the Viability of Marketable Permits." Ph.D. dissertation, California Institute of Technology, Pasadena.

Hahn, R.W. 1981b. "Data Base and Programming Methodology for Marketable Permits Study." Open File Report No. 80-8. Environmental Quality Laboratory, California Institute of Technology, Pasadena.

Hahn, R.W., and R.G. Noll 1982. "Implementing Tradable Emissions Permits." In *Reforming the New Social Regulation,* edited by LeRoy Gramer. Beverly Hills: Sage Publications.

Montgomery, W.D. 1972. "Markets in Licenses and Efficient Pollution Control Programs." *Journal of Economic Theory* 5(December):395–418.

Roberts, M.J., and M. Spence. 1976. "Effluent Charges and Licenses Under Uncertainty." *Journal of Public Economics* 5:193–208.

Teitenberg, T.H. 1980. "Transferable Discharge Permits and the Control of Stationary Source Air Pollution: A Survey and Synthesis." *Land Economics* 56:391–416.

8 WHO LOSES FROM REFORM OF ENVIRONMENTAL REGULATION?

David Harrison, Jr. and Paul R. Portney

Why do economically efficient government programs or policies often encounter fierce opposition? One reason, as any student of public policy knows, concerns the distribution of benefits and costs. Even though the benefits of a program may exceed the associated costs, many of those affected by the policy—perhaps even the majority—may be left worse off. Even those who do not lose may object to a precipitous change in policy.

For reasons of politics and fairness, then, it may be necessary or desirable to compensate those who suffer net losses as a result of a policy change. When the landmark environmental laws of the early 1970s went into effect, for example, they incorporated several provisions offering implicit and explicit compensation to adversely affected parties. Although these mechanisms did not quiet the business and labor critics of environmental regulation, they did at least diminish complaints enough to allow for these major changes to occur.

Another change in environmental and other regulatory policies now under consideration is to use market-oriented or incentive-based approaches rather than legalistic and detailed guidelines.[1] Many of those seeking to reform federal environmental regulation also propose a shift from the current emphasis on preventing any adverse health-effects from pollution, to a requirement that health and other benefits be balanced against the costs of cleanup.[2] The reforms we discuss

147

here involve a greater role for economics both in establishing environmental standards and in determining how those standards are to be met. There will be losers, of course, from implementing this approach to environmental regulation. However, little thought has gone into identifying these groups or devising appropriate compensation for them.

COMPENSATION IN THE CURRENT SYSTEM

Those who lose from government policy changes are usually compensated out of political necessity. When Congress planned to expand California's Redwood National Park, for example, the loggers who would lose their jobs as a result of diminished timber production constituted a vocal and easily identifiable group of losers. To secure their acquiescence, Congress therefore included a system of payments in the proposal. This system offered the loggers an average of $6,000 per week during the early part of the compensation program.[3] Similarly, in its efforts to break down barriers to international trade, Congress immediately faced the problem of cushioning the blow to domestic workers in the shoe, textile, and other industries affected by removal of regulatory protection. The congressional response was to pass the Trade Adjustment Assistance Act, which provided supplements to regular unemployment compensation when joblessness resulted from lowered trade barriers. The program was later extended to workers hurt by import competition, even if no trade barriers had existed.

Business groups are also often offered compensation when the government wants to implement policy changes. For instance, when the Interstate Commerce Commission began to relax restrictions on entry to new trucking routes, the value of certificates for those routes fell substantially. As part of the Reagan Administration's 1981 tax cut bill, trucking companies were therefore allowed to write off as losses any diminution in the market value of their certificates resulting from deregulation, thereby compensating affected owners for some effects of deregulation.[4]

Compensation in the wake of policy change is common in the environmental arena. When the Clean Air and Clean Water Acts were amended significantly in the early 1970s, Congress created at the same time several forms of compensation to ease the transition to more stringent regulations. Interestingly, perhaps the most explicit form of compensation incorporated in these two acts benefits neither firms nor workers. It is directed instead to state and local governments. Title II of the Clean Water Act established a major federal subsidy for constructing municipal sewage treatment plants that would meet various technology-based standards. The federal subsidy covers 75 percent (and in certain cases 85 percent) of the cost of constructing these facilities. Through 1980, the Environmental Protection Agency (EPA) expended more than $20 billion in such subsidies. This large public works program no doubt contributed to the political support for the clean water effort.[5]

To ease the burden that environmental regulation imposes on the private sector, Congress also permits firms to finance pollution control equipment by tax-exempt Industrial Development Bonds, one of the few cases in which private companies have access to the tax-exempt bond market. The interest paid to bond holders is tax free, enabling firms (acting through quasi-public pollution control financing agencies) to offer lower interest rates on the bonds. In 1980, for example, the yield on tax-exempt bonds was about 9 percent, while that on comparable and taxable corporate bonds was about 13 percent. In 1979 and 1980, tax-free bonds financed $2.9 billion in pollution control equipment (Lulkovich 1981). Although the savings to companies that result are small relative to the costs of complying with the Clean Air Act and Clean Water Acts,[6] the tax-exempt provisions clearly provide some financial relief to firms adversely affected by federal enviornmental regulation.

Direct compensation to workers harmed by environmental regulation is much more limited than that extended to the redwood loggers or to those affected by the foreign imports mentioned above. EPA does, however, employ an early warning system that is supposed to alert it as well as other federal agencies to potential job losses and plant closing that may be due to regulatory policies. Although EPA provides no financial assistance (or jobs) to affected parties, it does offer information to workers, firms, and communities about other possibilities for federal assistance, such as from the Small Business Administration or the Economic Development Administration. In addition, EPA alerts these agencies to possible demands on their resources.

Workers do receive more indirect kinds of compensation from many environmental laws. Most regulation imposes stricter discharge standards on new sources of pollution than existing sources. The increased burden on new sources has a political logic. Those hurt by strict new-source controls are those who do not get a job they might have gotten in the future. But if controls are imposed on existing sources, some individuals already holding jobs may be harmed—which creates many more political problems. Similarly, the dates that environmental regulations are to take effect are often set in the future to allow firms and municipalities time to accommodate. On several occasions, Congress has extended deadlines still further when, as in the case of the automobile manufacturers, firms insisted they were neither technologically nor financially capable of meeting the standards at the prescribed time (Seskin 1978). Delays in effective dates save money for firms and therefore help facilitate the transition to a regulated state.

Perhaps the most important accommodation in both air and water pollution control laws is that emissions requirements must be economically achievable. In practice, this means that discharge standards for industries cannot be set at such a stringent level that an average (or perhaps model) plant would close or lay off substantial numbers of workers. Even when a comparison of environmental benefits and abatement costs might justify additional controls on a particular industry, such controls would not be required if they are not affordable.

The intended beneficiaries of the economic achievability provisions are presumably the workers who might have lost their jobs had more stringent regulations been imposed. It is difficult to determine how effective the provision has been, however, because it is impossible to know how many jobs would have been lost without this constraint. Through mid-1979, however, EPA claims that only 24,478 workers were unemployed as a result of environmentally-related closures of 132 plants.[7]

Environmental statutes sometimes provide more focused protection or compensation. For example, one provision the Clean Air Act requires that all new or substantially modified coal-fired power plants remove some percentage of the sulfur contained in their boiler fuel, regardless of its initial sulfur content. As Ackerman and Hassler (1981) point out, the requirement was designed to discourage electric utilities from using low-sulfur coal to meet clean air standards, since this may have caused some unemployment among midwestern miners of high-sulfur coal. In addition, Section 125 of the Clean Air Act permits a governor or the president to prohibit use of nonlocally produced fuels in meeting national air quality goals. This protects the local coal mining jobs that would have been lost if an air polluter were allowed to import low-sulfur coal to meet State Implementation Plan (SIP) requirements (White 1981).

In summary, current environmental laws are replete with provisions that add neither to environmental benefits nor to the efficiency of control, but instead compensate the potential losers resulting from regulatory change. Many of the most economically irrational provisions—for example, differential treatment of old and new sources, use of affordability criteria to set emission standards, and public works subsidies—are thus accommodations for those who would be adversely affected by more stringent environmental laws. As such, they are part of the political price of achieving change.

LOSERS FROM REFORMS

Economic efficiency, of course, is not the only criteria by which to judge proposed regulatory reforms, and the alternatives discussed here are not the only options (Harrison and Portney, forthcoming). However, since the use of economic principles in environmental rule-making has been a mainstay of the economists' plea for reform, and because there is some reason to believe economic approaches will become more important in the current administration, the reforms considered in this paper all have economic efficiency as their principal objective.

Efficiency gains from reform—and the identification of losers—will depend upon the choice of approach and how it is implemented. This section identifies four major categories of economics-based regulatory reform, including: (1) current EPA reforms; (2) cost-effectiveness tests; (3) cost-benefit tests; and (4) economic incentive schemes. The categories are ordered in terms of increasing potential efficiency gains. The number of identifiable losers, and therefore the need for accommodation, also tends to increase as one proceeds from category (1) to category (4).

Current EPA Reforms

In recent years EPA has modified its regulatory approach in several ways to reduce the overall costs of pollution control without compromising environmental quality. Referring to these changes as "controlled trading," EPA emphasizes both that the changes are in fact trades rather than reductions in overall control, and that they are controlled by agency procedures and personnel.

The controlled trading reforms contain three major elements: (1) bubble policy; (2) offset policy; and (3) offset banking policy. Published in December 1979, the bubble policy allows a firm to increase its airborne emissions at one operation (e.g., a stack) if it makes at least as great a reduction elsewhere (e.g., at another stack or a process). Firms cannot trade for greater emissions at their new sources under the bubble policy, as the bubble policy only applies to standards imposed by states on existing plants.

A firm can make use of the offset policy, however, to locate a new plant in an area that does not meet required ambient air quality standards. The offset policy was developed in 1976, when it appeared that the Clean Air Act requirements might prohibit new pollution sources in the "nonattainment" areas. EPA proposed allowing new construction in such areas on the condition that the new source offset its pollution by reducing levels elsewhere, either at its existing plant or at nearby plants owned by other firms. This policy became part of the Clean Air Act in the 1977 amendments.

The banking policy extends the possibility of trades or offsets to emissions reductions that have already occurred. A firm that reduces its emissions below the permitted level may "bank" the excess reductions for later use in expansion or bubbles, or they may sell their "credit" to some other firm. Banking thus provides an incentive for a firm to reduce emissions beyond current requirements even if it has no trades of its own to make.

Among the limitations of EPA's controlled trading reforms is the fact that firms wanting to use the bubble or offset policies must overcome substantial administrative obstacles. In addition, if EPA tightens future emission standards, the advantages from trades may eventually be lost. Finally, all water pollutants and some air pollutants cannot be traded.

From the perspective of this chapter, however, the EPA reforms have the important advantage of not creating any losers in the polluting industries. If a given firm takes advantage of a bubble trade or an offset transaction, no other firm's control requirements increase. Even the transactions costs are taken into account. Since a firm must apply for the trade, it can determine for itself whether the added administrative costs or uncertainty created by the transaction exceed the likely savings.

Indirect losses, however, might arise from the trades. Pollution control equipment makers may lose if firms substitute process changes for end-of-pipe control. If trades in fact compromise air quality, another group that may lose is environmentalists. For example, critics of a proposal for a Virginia refinery protested that offsets planned for several miles from the proposed construction would do nothing to improve the air quality locally (Clark 1979). Competitors of firms that use trades to reduce costs may lose if the cost advantage from the trade is substantial. Finally, the trading firms themselves may lose if, as mentioned above, EPA tightens future emission standards based upon information from the trades. Since the firm would no longer be able to claim the credit for lower emissions, this possibility is equivalent to confiscating the gains from trades. Although firms that actually make the trades are most vulnerable, other firms in the industry with similar emissions control systems may also face more stringent standards. The possibility for confiscation thus makes the legal status of the trade, especially its duration, particularly important.

Cost-Effectiveness Tests

The basic rule for minimizing the cost of achieving given emissions reductions is to equalize the marginal cost per pound of emissions removed among various sources. Many provisions of environmental legislation, however, have the effect of increasing the costs to society above the minimum, the economic achievability criterion being a primary example. If a cost-effectiveness test were used, new and old sources of pollutants would be regulated equally, and cost-per-pound-removed calculations would replace affordability as the basis for setting emissions standards.

Adopting cost-effectiveness tests would represent a major extension of the controlled trading reforms. All emissions could, in effect, be traded. There would be no restrictions for firms with a single emission source, for the emissions above new source standards that cannot now be offset, and for the many pollutants, like water effluents, that cannot be traded at all. Compliance costs would thus be reduced below those under the controlled trading reforms. Administrative costs would also be lower, since EPA could use the information it has already collected on costs and emissions reductions rather than have firms go through the effort of establishing trades. Firms would also gain some greater certainty, since standards set by EPA would probably be less subject to change than banked or traded emissions.

Employing cost-effective standards is therefore likely to reduce the overall resource cost of current environmental quality improvements. The results of a recent study by Battelle Laboratories, substantially revised by EPA, suggest the potential savings from such a measure. The incremental cost-effectiveness estimates calculated for both air and water pollution controls in six industries indicate that cost-per-ton-removed of particulates varies from $55 to $2,243 (EPA 1981).

Despite their impeccable logic, cost-effectiveness tests are open to serious criticism. Some objections would no doubt come from environmental groups suspicious that cost-effective regulation would in fact mean less effective regulation. Such groups may therefore consider themselves indirect losers from any change that introduces cost-effectiveness into the rulemaking process. Pollution control equipment manufacturers may also feel threatened if demand for their products decreases.[8] The most important drawback of cost-effectiveness tests, however, is that they generate direct losers. Supporters of cost-effectiveness usually emphasize the advantages of avoiding control where it will be expensive, pointing out that a firm with high control costs will clearly gain when a cost-effective test is applied. If total cleanup is to remain the same in the prereform and reform situations, however, some firms' control requirements will have to increase if others are cut back. Unless compensated, those whose requirements increase are direct losers from regulatory reform.

Firms with low per unit compliance costs, high volumes of wastes, and little ability to pass control costs on to consumers are the most likely to be direct losers from cost-effectiveness reform. Because many regulatory standards are generally based on "ability to afford" compliance costs, firms and industries that cannot pass costs on—either because they are marginal firms or because they face substantial foreign competition—typically operate under less stringent environmental regulations.

A recent controversy over setting industrial water pollution standards illustrates the attitude of potential losers from cost-effectiveness reform (Harrison and Leone, forthcoming). In 1977, Congress modified criteria for so-called conventional pollutants by substituting Best Conventional Technology (BCT) standards for Best Available

Technology (BAT). The BCT standards take into account the "reasonableness of control costs," using the costs for municipal wastewater treatment as a standard of reasonableness. In August 1979, EPA established a benchmark of $1.15 per pound of pollutants removed, in effect requiring cost-effective standards. If incremental BAT control costs are above $1.15 per pound, the standard must be weakened enough to lower the costs to $1.15 per pound.

The principal opponent of the EPA's handling of BCT standards has been the pulp and paper industry, which generates enormous volumes of waterborne wastes in its production processes. A plant that produces 600 tons of pulp per day and directly employs 700 workers would use 40 million gallons of water each day.[9] The used wash-water places a demand on the receiving waters equal to the sewage of a city of one million people. On a per unit basis, these wastes are relatively inexpensive to treat because of the economies of scale associated with such large water volumes. In part because American pulp and paper companies face stiff competition from Canadian firms, however, water effluent standards have been less stringent than if cost-effectiveness were the major criterion. Virtually all of the additional control options currently available would be reasonable under the current EPA benchmark of $1.15 per pound. Thus, while the overall costs of controlling conventional water pollution would decrease if the benchmark generated the same total level of control as before, control costs for firms in the pulp and paper industry would increase. It is therefore not surprising that the industry has been actively seeking to persuade EPA to adopt a lower benchmark.

From the standpoint of control requirements, a cost-effectiveness test represents a zero-sum game: for every firm whose emission control target is decreased, another firm's target is increased.[10] Since by definition it is the high-cost firm whose requirements are eased, the plan, of course, is not a zero-sum game from the standpoint of costs. Although an economist would be quick to point out that the gainers could compensate the losers, in most cases, no such compensation occurs. Losers remain losers despite the overall societal gain.

Cost-Benefit Analysis

Cost-effectiveness reforms implicitly assume agreement over environmental objectives—either overall emissions reductions or improvements in ambient quality. Such reforms can thus provide efficiency gains in the small, that is, lower the cost of achieving given goals. Cost-benefit analysis, however, raises the issue of whether the goals are in fact appropriate.

Many environmental statutes adopt criteria for setting goals that preclude the weighing of costs and benefits. Among the more well-known examples are the mandate of the Clean Air Act that national ambient air quality standards be set to protect the public health with an adequate margin of safety, and the goal of the Clean Water Act that all the nation's waters be fishable and swimmable in 1983 and free of discharges by 1985. Many commentators (e.g., Harrison and Portney 1981) have argued that these statutes should be modified to permit at least rough comparisons of the costs and benefits of control.

Executive Order 12291, the Reagan Administration's blueprint for regulatory reform, strongly encourages the use of cost-benefit analyses. The order requires every regulatory agency to prepare a Regulatory Impact Analysis that, among other things, includes "a determination of the potential net benefits of the rule, including an evaluation of the effects that cannot be quantified in monetary terms." Section 2(c) of the Executive Order also mandates that "regulatory objectives shall be chosen to maximize the net benefits to society." Whether agencies will use cost-benefit tests to establish major regulations depends upon whether the statute under which they regulate permits such a test and, if so, whether the agency chooses to use its discretion to promote the criterion.

Basing regulatory choices on costs and benefits would provide all of the efficiency benefits lacking in the current EPA reforms. All emissions could, in effect, be traded, even between different pollutants. Given the disregard for costs in much environmental legislation, however, such reform will often result in fewer and less stringent environmental regulations, the major exception being where justifiable regulations are not affordable. This relaxation of standards would in turn generate many clearly identifiable winners, that is, businesses relieved of regulatory burdens.

The use of cost-benefit principles is likely to create additional losers as well. Firms or industries that currently gain from the disregard for differences in the benefits of control would lose if cost-benefit analyses were required. As mentioned, many environmental standards (e.g., new source performance standards for air polluants) are uniform for all firms in an industry or industry subcategory. Emissions from some firms, however, are much more damaging than others, typically because they affect more people. A new plant in New York City, for example, would do much more damage than the same plant located in upstate New York. If agencies had discretion to set standards based on comparisons of costs and benefits, the New York City plant would face much stiffer controls than one in upstate New York. While the current uniform requirements are justified by the need to prevent firms from basing their locational choices on the stringency of environmental controls, from a cost-benefit perspective these are indeed the grounds on which to choose a site.

Consider the example of EPA's proposed regulations requiring a 97 percent reduction in benzene emissions from maleic anhydride plants.[11] Table 8-1 lists the estimated benefits and costs of controlling the eight plants that use benzene as a feedstock, and therefore are subject to this regulation. Controls on one plant, St. Louis Monsanto, provide over 80 percent of projected health benefits from the proposed standards. Benefits are especially high because Monsanto is one of three plants operating without controls and because the area around the plants is densely populated. The importance of plant-

Table 8-1. Annualized Costs and Benefits of 97 Percent Control at Individual Maleic Anhydride Plants.

	Current Control (%)	Annual Cost ($1,000)	Annual Leukemia Deaths Prevented
Monsanto	0	542-669	0.033
Reichhold (Ill.)	90	320-402	0.00036
U.S. Steel	90	547-677	0.0140
Reichhold (N.J.)	97	0	0.00647
Tenneco	0	213-273	0.00458
Denka	97	0	0.0082
Ashland	0	410-498	0.000845
Koppers	99	0	0.0020
Total cost ($/year)		2,032-2,519	
Total benefit (deaths/year)			0.0705

Source: Harrison (1981).

specific considerations are also clear from Table 8-2, which presents estimates of the cost per leukemia death averted for several different groupings of the plants. The cost per death averted is much lower for controls on the Monsanto plant than for the other two plant groupings. The ratio is one-fifth that for the two plants currently operating without controls, and one-fiftieth that for plants operating with controls.

Although a strong case for setting different standards for the various plants (or at least for different groups of plants) therefore exists, such a system would create large winners and losers within the maleic anhydride industry. While uniform standards do create winners and losers as well (Leone and Jackson 1981), the differences are only magnified under a cost-benefit test. Losers in such a situation may represent a much greater practical obstacle to instituting cost-benefit considerations in environmental rulemaking than the methodological and data difficulties. Residents around the low-control plants may also object. When source-by-source standards based on benefits and costs replace uniform standards, some sources will be allowed to relax controls. A maleic anhydride plant in a sparsely populated region, for example, might be able to lower standards since the benefits of control may be small. Those who do reside near the plant, however, will no doubt protest the removal of protection because a cost-benefit analysis determines that it is uneconomical. They may demand the

Table 8-2. Estimated Incremental Cost-Benefit Ratios under Several Regulatory Alternatives (million dollars per leukemia death averted).

	No Regulation to BAT (97% control)	90% Control to BAT (97% control)	BAT (97% control) to 99% Control
Monsanto plant (no controls)	1.62–2.00	—	1.53–23.4
Tenneco and Ashland plants (no controls)	11.2–11.9	—	—
U.S. Steel, Reichhold (Ill.) (currently controlling to 90%)	—	114.4–142.3	—
Seven other plants (without Monsanto)	—	73.0–102.8	75.4–191.7

Source: Harrison (1981).

same protection afforded their big-city counterparts, even though it might not make the same economic sense.

Economic Incentive Schemes

While the precise advantages of economic incentive schemes depend upon a number of factors (uncertainty over benefits, competitiveness of firms, and so forth), many commentators (e.g., Baumol and Oates 1979) regard regulatory reform as synonymous with the substitution of economic incentive schemes for command-and-control regulation. The virtue of an incentive approach is that it decentralizes decision-making. Rather than have the government establish control levels for each firm under the cost-benefit rule, an effluent charge or a marketable permits scheme would allow firms to determine their pollution output just as they determine their production levels. In addition, economic incentives offer better, or at least more concrete, inducements to develop more cost-effective control methods.

Although the case for economic incentives is well established, there are no examples of such schemes in operation. The five recent empirical studies listed in Table 8–3, however, discuss implementation of incentive schemes that address the major types of environmental disamenities. Three of these analyses concentrate on marketable permits, one—aircraft noise—concentrates on effluent charges, and one—nitrous oxides (NO_x)—devotes equal attention to both. The strategies would operate on the national—aircraft noise and chlorofluorocarbons (CFCs)—the state—phosphates—and the local—NO_x, aircraft noise, and sulfur oxides (SO_x)—levels. The air pollutant examples focus on two pollutants that have been regulated for some time (NO_x and SO_x), and one that has recently become a source of concern (CFCs, linked to depletion of the ozone layer).

These studies all demonstrate the possible efficiency gains economic incentive schemes can provide relative to command-and-control approaches. For purposes of our present discussion these studies also provide information on the groups that may lose if economic incentives replace the current regulatory regime.

Business as a whole.   A fundamental difference between economic incentive schemes and the regulatory reforms discussed above is in the property rights they presume. Even stringent discharge standards

Table 8-3. Recent Empirical Studies of Economic Incentive Schemes.

Reference	Pollutant	Scheme(s)	Geographic Area	Issues Considered
David et al. (1977)	Water/ Phosphate	Marketable Permits	Wisconsin	Cost savings Income transfer
Palmer et al. (1980)	Air/CFC	Marketable Permits	United States	Cost savings Income transfer
Anderson et al. (1979)	Air/NO$_x$	Marketable Permits Emission Charges	Chicago	Cost savings Geographic variation Income transfer
Harrison (forthcoming)	Aircraft Noise	Emission Charges Marketable Permits	United States and Boston's Logan Airport	Cost savings Geographic variation Income transfer
Hahn and Noll (Chapter 7)	Air/SO$_x$	Marketable Permits	Los Angeles	Geographic variation Income transfer Market power

usually permit some pollution, thereby implying that the source(s) "own" some amount. Under the standard effluent charge scheme or marketable permits scheme, polluters must pay for all their emissions.[12] Business may, of course, pass some or all the costs on to customers or labor in the form of higher product prices or lower wages. Like the excise taxes they resemble, the fraction passed on will depend upon industry cost and market conditions.[13] Nevertheless, these payments probably explain why business has failed to support economic incentive schemes. (Since few schemes have been seriously considered, outright opposition has not been necessary.)

Since payments allow government purchases or tax reductions, the permit costs or effluent taxes incurred by business, or their customers and employees, are of course transfers rather than real resource costs. The five empirical studies listed in Table 8–3 demonstrate that the sums at question are far from trivial. The Rand study of chlorofluorocarbons (Palmer et al. 1980), for example, reports the largest transfer from polluters to the regulatory authority. The present value of transfer payments from a national CFC permit system for the decade 1980 to 1990 is estimated to be between $1.15 and $1.7 billion (1976 dollars). Harrison (forthcoming) estimates that introduction of a national aircraft noise charge scheme with a baseline (no charge level) of 98 decibels would generate about $150 million per year in revenue. Revenues would decrease over time as noisy aircraft are retired from the fleet.

The wealth transfers estimated in the other studies are even more dramatic since they occur from local rather than national schemes. For instance, in Chapter 7 Hahn and Noll estimate the potential income transfer from a Los Angeles SO_x market at $150 million per year (the range is from $65 million to $250 million), or an average of $15 per Los Angeles resident. For a potential NO_x market in Chicago, Mathtech (Anderson et al. 1979) estimates that transfers could range from $5.4 million to as much as $468 million per year. Harrison reports that a noise charge levied at Boston's Logan Airport might generate $38 million per year, which would be an 80 percent increase in Logan's total revenue. While these schemes are local, the final burdens of the income transfers would be likely to fall on consumers and stockholders outside the area.

Businesses, and society, obviously stand to gain if the change from command-and-control regulation to economic incentives permits firms to use cheaper means of pollution abatement. Whether the payments for previously "free" pollution cancel out these savings depends upon several factors, including the variation in marginal costs, the stringency of controls, and the inefficiency of the previous control requirements.

The empirical studies provide some information on the relative importance of compliance costs and transfer payments in different regulatory situations. The water pollution and CFC studies illustrate the two extreme cases. The marginal cost of removing phosphorus from Lake Michigan is graphed in Figure 8–1. Transfer payments are relatively small because municipalities are required to remove 85 percent of the phosphorus, and thus only 15 percent was previously "owned" by cities that must now buy permits. Compliance costs are substantially greater. In contrast, under the benchmark CFC control strategy that Rand evaluated, in which CFC emissions are only reduced by about 15 percent, a firm's expenses for transfers under the permit policy are about fourteen times the costs of actually reducing emissions. Only a few CFC-using firms have compliance costs that exceed the permit payments (assuming that all permits are originally government owned).

Individual firms.   Economic incentive schemes create the same gains and losses among firms as the cost-effectiveness and cost-benefit tests. Firms with low control costs have compliance cost increases while firms finding control expensive have decreases. Although the net effect is to reduce overall costs, the low cost compliers are likely to consider the results of economic incentive schemes unfair.

The empirical studies also provide a sense of the quantitative importance of the reallocations that might occur under an economic incentive scheme as compared to mandatory controls. The results from the CFC study presented in Table 8–4 indicate that while overall compliance costs fall by 58 percent under a hypothetical permit scheme, compliance costs increase by $21.6 million for makers of solvents, a 25 percent increase from costs under mandatory controls. However, the decrease in costs for the other two major emitters are even more dramatic: Compliance costs for flexible foam and rigid foam are 70 percent and 90 percent lower, respectively. Solvent manufacturers are nonetheless likely to have little enthusiasm for the permit scheme.

If an aircraft noise charge scheme were in effect, compliance costs increases for some airlines would be even greater than for solvent makers. In Table 8–5 are estimates of the noise charges that would be

Figure 8-1. Total Removal versus Cost of Efficient Treatment for Lake Michigan Basin.

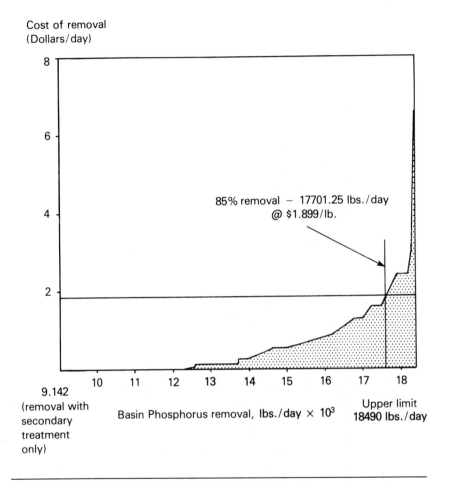

Cost of removal
(Dollars/day)

85% removal — 17701.25 lbs./day
@ $1.899/lb.

9.142
(removal with
secondary
treatment
only)

Basin Phosphorus removal, lbs./day × 10³

Upper limit
18490 lbs./day

Source: David et al. (1977).

assessed against airlines using Boston's Logan Airport, assuming current flight schedules. These estimates overstate costs since introduction of a noise charge is likely to result in fewer flights, especially at night, and in quieter aircraft. The figures do, however, suggest the potential for large cost increases. For example, charges for Flying Tiger Airlines would increase over a thousand-fold if the weight-based landing fee is supplemented by a noise charge. American Airlines'

Table 8-4. Changes in Compliance Costs for Industries under a CFC Marketable Permit Scheme.

| Product Area | Cumulative Effects of Economic Incentives | | Deviation from Mandatory Controls | |
	Emissions Reduction (millions of permit pounds)	Compliance Cost	Emissions Reduction (millions of permit pounds)	Compliance Cost
Flexible Foam	380.7	29.2	− 120.5	− 64.1
Solvents	390.3	67.3	+ 204.6	+ 21.6
Rigid Foam	26.7	3.8	− 79.4	− 35.0
Retail Food	18.3	7.3	—	—
Chillers	1.0	0.1	—	—
Total	816.9	107.8	+ 4.6	− 77.5

Source: Palmer et al. (1980: 223).

Table 8-5. Estimated Noise Charges at Logan Airport for Fiscal Year 1977.

Airline	Landing Fee ($)	Noise Charge ($)	Total ($)	Percent Change	Airline's Landing Fee as % of Total of All Landing Fees	Airline's Total Fees as % Of Total of All Landing Fees and Noise Charges	Change (Increased % Burden)
American	2,173,996	9,984,829	12,158,825	+459	16.4	23.9	+7.5
Allegheny	1,209,183	4,167,095	5,376,278	345	9.1	10.5	+1.4
Delta	2,620,628	5,463,467	8,084,095	208	19.8	15.9	-3.9
Eastern	2,357,921	6,705,734	9,063,655	284	17.8	17.8	—
Flying Tiger	132,298	1,496,284	1,628,582	1131	1.0	3.2	+2.2
National	95,372	128,676	224,048	135	0.7	0.4	-0.3
North Central	56,988	69,552	126,540	122	0.4	0.2	-0.2
Northwest	142,295	231,253	373,548	163	1.1	0.7	-0.4
Pan Am	353,202	242,414	595,616	67	2.7	1.2	-1.5
Seaboard	68,367	158,688	227,053	232	0.5	0.4	-0.1
TWA	1,604,264	4,318,002	5,922,266	269	12.1	11.6	-0.5
United	945,731	3,635,090	4,580,821	384	7.1	9.0	+1.9
Air Canada	184,256	196,560	380,816	107	1.4	0.8	-0.6
Air France	83,738	84,032	167,770	100	0.6	0.3	-0.3
Alitalia	75,322	40,560	115,882	54	0.6	0.2	-0.4
British Airways	262,781	147,056	409,837	56	2.0	0.8	-1.2
Irish (Aer Lingus)	72,904	113,568	186,472	156	0.5	0.4	-0.1
Lufthansa	247,311	178,464	425,775	72	1.9	0.8	-1.1
Swissair	249,745	355,082	604,827	142	1.9	1.2	-0.7
TAP	46,789	37,856	84,645	81	0.8	0.2	-0.1
Air New England	162,625	—	162,625	0	1.2	0.3	-0.9
Commuter Carriers	112,028	—	112,028	0	0.9	0.2	-0.7
Total	13,257,744	37,754,260	51,012,004	285	100.0	100.0	0.0

Source: Harrison (forthcoming).

charges would grow by 459 percent. Even if the total revenue collected remained the same, the shares that different airlines pay would change dramatically.

In some cases, economic incentive schemes may impose costs on firms or municipalities whose emissions were previously ignored by the regulatory system. In the Lake Michigan case, for example, Wisconsin regulations exempted small towns (with populations less than 2,500) from discharge requirements, even though such towns emitted almost 25 percent of the phosphorus permitted to enter the basin. Under the proposed marketable permit scheme, these exempted communities would share the costs of abatement (although they may not end up reducing effluent if they are high-cost compliers and thus purchasers of permits). The same changes might occur for owners or operators of nonjet aircraft, whose noise emissions are not currently controlled.

Although the NO_x study does not break down compliance costs or charge (permit) costs by firm or industry, the authors do report some results of differential charges for three sources of NO_x. Charges are higher for sources located in dirtier areas because of the requirement that all parts of the urban area meet ambient air quality standards and the greater reductions needed where clean air is more scarce. The three rates are as follows:

Source Category	Charge Rate ($/lb of NO_x/hr)
Industrial coal-fired boilers	8,300
Industrial oil and gas fired boilers	25,000
Industrial process units	13,333

While these differential standards make sense from an efficiency standpoint, owners of industrial oil- and gas-fired boilers may object to their higher charges.

Other groups.   The political obstacles to adopting economic incentive schemes may come from other groups that have a stake in the environmental regulation. As with other types of economics-based schemes, environmentalists may oppose the reform if they expect economic incentives to generate less environmental improvement. State and local officials may also oppose the schemes if they complicate pollution control or increase administrative burdens. Of course, opposition is highly sensitive to the particular case. In some circumstances, the schemes may be perceived as providing greater environmental benefits or facilitating administrative processes. For example, economic incentive schemes may reduce administrative burdens by eliminating costly confrontations between agencies and regulated firms. The impersonal nature of the permit scheme, in particular, may therefore be appealing to regulatory officials.

Most of the empirical studies provide little information on the likely attitudes of other groups toward incentive schemes. The Harrison study of aircraft noise does, however, examine the perspective of an individual airport operator. The analysis indicates that while a noise charge has advantages from a national perspective, it has many disadvantages for the airport operator. The major drawback is that the charge creates uncertainties about the level of noise control achieved as well as about how noise will be reduced. The airport operator is likely to be particularly concerned about the possibility of airlines reducing flights and thereby jeopardizing the airport's role in maintaining a healthy local or regional economy. The operator may also want to have a greater control over the level of noise reduction than is possible under a charge scheme, at least initially.

Other objections may be even more diffuse. Part of the resistance to introducing economic incentive schemes may be due to the conviction that pollution control should not be left to quasi-market institutions (Kelman 1981). While most economic commentators deride the criticism of economic incentive schemes as licenses to pollute— regulations permitting a specified amount of pollution are no more or less so—this sense of distrust may constitute a political obstacle. This attitude is particularly important because the efficiency benefits of charge or permit schemes are ultimately so diffuse that they do not generate strong political support. Since individual consumers have little to gain from a switch to more efficient pollution control, they may consider the gain forgone a small price to pay for "principle."

ACCOMMODATIONS TO LOSERS
FROM REFORMS

Like any change in the regulatory system, then, a shift to economic principles for setting environmental standards may produce losers.

This section focuses primarily on the effects of implementing economic incentive schemes, not because such schemes are the most likely to be adopted, but because they offer the greatest potential efficiency gains and generate the most pronounced losers. They also offer the greatest opportunities for accommodation. Unlike cost-effectiveness or cost-benefit tests, fee and permit schemes allow authorities to alter the pattern of losses with relatively straightforward modifications. Those changes, however, may imply some compromises in efficiency.

Controlled Trading

The simple logic of EPA's controlled trading reforms—that firms should be able to reallocate pollution control among their various plants if they can save money and maintain the same environmental impact—suggests that there are no losers in this system. There are three major potential losers, however—equipment manufacturers, environmentalists, and polluters. Pollution equipment manufacturers would be most difficult to accommodate, but also the least likely to suffer harm. Under the bubble and other controlled trading schemes, changes in demand for equipment will be gradual and firms would likely adapt to reduced demand with relatively smooth transitions for both capital and labor.

Environmentalists may lose from these reforms if trades are in fact unequal. Environmentalists fear that polluters will use bubble trades to delay compliance, confuse enforcement, or substitute control of less important for more important pollutants. For example, EPA was concerned that Armco Steel's proposal to substitute control of road dust for stack emissions control would not only make enforcement more difficult, but also generate more of the fine particulates that appear to be more damaging to health. The original trading guidelines accommodated many of the environmentalists' objections by requiring detailed reviews and restrictions on trades. Although procedures were relaxed somewhat at the end of the Carter Administration, current requirements still seem to pose minor threats to air and water quality objectives.

If EPA or the states use information on cost savings from trades to increase the stringency of control, polluters could suffer losses. It is certainly possible that states will eventually revise their implementation plans to place more stringent controls on firms that demonstrate they can achieve greater emissions reductions at relatively modest costs. A guarantee that control requirements would not be changed for a fixed period, however, would reduce the potential losses to traders. Unlike some other accommodations, this guarantee would increase the efficiency of the trading system since more firms would participate if their savings were secure. Guarantees may, however, force states to use more costly means of reducing emissions in the next round of plan revisions.

One other category of potential loser under the controlled trading scheme is state and local environmental agencies. These agencies must cope with changes in administrative requirements and negotiate with polluters over many details of emissions control. They are likely to object to any additional flexibility in requirements, even if the options reduce the overall social cost of pollution control. EPA has been sensitive to the needs of these officials, however, and has developed a well-staffed program to explain the opportunities and the procedures of controlled trading to state and local officials, as well as businesses. In the present context, these actions represent accommodations to potential losers under the controlled trading system, thus increasing political support for the program.

Cost-Effectiveness and Cost-Benefit Tests

Polluters, in general, may well gain from any change to cost-effectiveness or cost-benefit tests. Overall compliance costs will, by definition, be lower under a cost-effectiveness plan, and cost-benefit principles will probably result in less ambitious environmental quality goals. Individual firms, however, will fare quite differently. Firms with high volumes of waste, relatively low control costs, and little ability to pass on added costs to consumers will clearly pay a larger share of total costs, and perhaps even higher absolute costs. In addition, under the cost-benefit tests, firms operating in large, dense areas or areas with special environmental importance will face more stringent standards.

How can these losses be accommodated? Not very easily. As stated above, the current system includes many provisions to accommodate losers from strict environmental statutes. Although affordability or technical feasibility criteria have not made environmental controls popular with business, they may at least have made controls politically feasible. Changing to a more efficient criterion for setting standards, however, does not provide any degree of freedom to accommodate the political process.

As noted above, some individuals could suffer more exposure to harmful substances if standard-setting were determined on a cost-benefit rather than a prevent-all-harm basis. Potential losses could be avoided, however, especially if the firms' savings from the reform were large enough. Firms might pay for relocation and added transportation expenses, or offer employees and others living near the plant preventive health care.

Economic Incentive Schemes

Economic incentive schemes create some of the same losers—for example, equipment manufacturers, environmentalists, and high-volume polluters—as other regulatory reforms. In addition, the transfer payments under the economic incentive systems create losses for business as a whole, losses shared among stockholders, workers, and customers. The recent empirical studies reviewed in the previous section indicate that these losses can be very large and, indeed, they may well outnumber the cost savings from removing inflexible and costly control requirements.

The economic incentive schemes, however, embody natural mechanisms for reducing or eliminating transfer payments. These methods create their own winners and losers among firms (and among firms and their customers) though, and also can create additional difficulties that may threaten some of the schemes' efficiency advantages. The marketable permits scheme provides the most obvious opportunity to reduce transfer payments from business to government. Rather than have the government auction off permits, the environmental agency can distribute permits to polluters. Property rights are split among polluters and the public, with firms "owning" the right to pollute up to the number of permits issued. The market then determines who actually performs the cleanup.

Effluent charge revenues can also be lowered either by setting the baseline higher than zero for the tax, or by combining subsidies with taxes. For example, the Harrison study of aircraft noise uses 98 decibels as the starting point for the noise charge, thereby reducing the airline payments dramatically. Creating a subsidy for noise from 98 decibels to 105 decibels and a charge for noise above 105 decibels could reduce the transfers even further. Alternatively, the regulatory authority could simply keep the revenues in a trust fund to be disbursed to polluting firms. Aircraft noise revenues could also be used to offset the ticket tax the government levies on all airlines.

Reducing transfers for polluters as a whole, then, is not difficult. The specific features of the scheme will, however, have a differential impact on individual firms. Discussed below are the two empirical studies that consider the effects of alternative allocation systems on "equity" among firms, and on overall efficiency.

CFC marketable permits study.[14] The Rand study of a marketable permits scheme estimated that auctioning off CFC permits would result in government revenues of over $2 billion between 1981 and 1990. The simplest method of redirecting transfer payments would be to allocate the permits to the five firms that manufacture CFCs based upon historical (1980) production. Although the administrative costs would therefore be small, the income transfers would be large. Estimates in Table 8-6 indicate that, for example, DuPont would receive permit rights worth over $1 billion during the ten-year period. Indeed, the Rand study concludes that CFC producers would be better off under the regulation because the wealth transfer exceeds any loss from reductions the quota causes in CFC production.

The Rand researchers refer to this historical allocation to producers as "neutral" since it does not affect the CFC manufacturers'

Table 8-6. CFC Producers' Transfers Receipts under Allocation by Estimated 1980 Market Shares.

Producer	Millions of Permits	Discounted Cumulative Receipts, 1981–89 (1978 $ × 10^6)
Allied	79.5	472.7
DuPont	197.4	1,173.8
Kaiser	25.0	148.7
Pennwalt	25.0	163.3
Racon	8.5	50.5
Total	338.2	2,011.1

Source: Palmer and Quinn (1981:42).

production costs or the amount users are willing to pay. A virtue of the neutral policy is that they do not distort efficient market responses to a quota. The permit allocations do not affect decisions to enter or leave an industry, to reduce or expand production, or to change production processes. Resource costs of the control program therefore do not increase. A drawback of the policy is that since pricing and production decisions are unchanged, only losses to producers are accommodated. Losses to CFC users, consumers and workers remain the same.

Because CFCs are a good—and not simply an unfortunate by-product like most pollutants—the permits can be allocated to firms that purchase (as opposed to produce) CFCs. While such an allocation formula spreads the transfers more widely, it also would be much more costly to administer. The number of CFC users is very large: over 140,000 firms install and service CFC-using mobile air conditioning units alone. Although calculating permit entitlements need be done only once (or once per decade), the large numbers of users make this system much more costly to administer than allocation to five CFC producers. If as many as 250,000 firms were eligible for permits and the cost of obtaining data and computing entitlements were $100 per firm, the administrative costs would be $25 million. Since the allocation to end-users is neutral, it does not distort resource allocation, but it also does not compensate losses to customers or workers.

The Rand study considers a nonneutral policy, as well. The "trickle-down" formula would change the permit allocation each year based upon the previous year's output, that is, a firm's share of final product output would determine its share of the total allocation. If a firm changed its output level relative to other regulated firms over the period, its permit allocation would also change. This allocation formula thus encourages firms to expand output, and thereby restrain increases in consumer prices and decreases in employment levels. The Rand researchers estimate that in 1985 the policy would eliminate about 76 percent of the increase in final product prices that would occur under the permit auction, while also reducing most of the short-term declines in output and employment levels.

As an illustration of the formula's effectiveness in compensating losers, the Rand researchers report the policy's impacts on the thermoformed polystyrene (TPS) industry. Under the auction plan, foam output is predicted to decline over 30 percent from 1981 to 1985. Under the final product formula, however, estimated TPS output is about 8 percent higher than in 1981. Thus, using this allocation formula eliminates worker layoffs during the first five years. Although industry output and employment may well decline after 1985, the formula clearly buys time during which workers can adjust to the new regulatory environment.

The two major drawbacks of the trickle-down formula are that it distorts choices and thus increases the costs of the quota, and it is administratively complex. Rand analyzed the inefficiencies created in both the permit and the final product markets. Because permits would allow firms to increase output and therefore qualify for larger allocations, the formula drives the price upward from $0.94 under the permit auction to $1.05. For CFC-related industries as a whole, compliance costs increase by $3.6 million per year (10.4 percent) with the trickle-down formula, although not all users experience cost increases. The final product formula also creates inefficiencies in resource allocation between CFC-related industries as a group and the rest of the economy because these industries expand output beyond efficient levels. Rand estimates that this loss costs another $2 million (5.8 percent) annually. The accommodation of losers thus adds nearly $6 million (a 16 percent increase) to the annual resource costs of the CFC quota.

Because the trickle-down formula requires the agency to acquire and assimilate data from thousands of CFC-user firms each year, it also entails higher administrative costs. Several complex problems arise that do not occur in the simpler schemes, for example, the questions of how to define and measure the output of each affected industry, devise the actual formula to convert changes in output into changes in permit allocations, and determine which firms would be eligible for allocations. Consider the issue of how to define qualifying output. Nearly identical final products can be produced with and without CFCs. Should all the product line be considered, or only the products now using CFCs? If only products now made with CFCs are included, the agency must develop specifications of the products so that they can be identified if no longer made with CFCs. This may be administratively difficult as well as costly. If all product lines are counted, however, the formula will subsidize some product markets that are not harmed by the CFC quota, and thereby reduce the compensation available to those actually harmed.

Los Angeles Sulfate Study.   Hahn and Noll (Chapter 7 of this book) emphasize that political feasibility and economic efficiency are design objectives rather than immutable characteristics of marketable rights schemes, and they discuss in detail the issues that arise in devising a marketable permits scheme that serves both objectives. A simple scheme in which the government auctions off sulfate rights would generate such large transfers relative to its efficiency gains that Hahn and Noll conclude that the principal focus of the political debate over alternative market designs would be wealth distribution rather than efficiency. Some initial allocation of the rights to polluters is necessary to avoid the transfer if the scheme is to be seriously considered.

Hahn and Noll discuss three bases for distributing permits that appear to have the strongest equity claims: emissions before recent control efforts (perhaps with some additional provisions for firms that entered or expanded capacity since then); emissions allowed under current controls; and projected emissions under a competitive, perfectly efficient market in permits. All three formulas have serious defects in terms of the efficiency of the permits market. Basing permits on the competitive equilibrium would tend to avoid the need for any transactions among present sources—although new sources and expansion would create demand for permits—and thus discourage the speedy attainment of a stable, competitive permit price.

Basing permit allocations on preregulatory or current control levels avoids the market thinness problem but creates the danger of market manipulation by one or a few firms. This possibility was considered a major problem in the Los Angeles case because one source (a utility) accounts for a large proportion of emissions and could have been the only buyer of permits. If the utility operated as a monopsonist, it would buy fewer permits at a lower price than under a competitive market and thus abate too much pollution. Additional abatement is worthwhile to the monopsonist because it would depress the price paid for permits it acquires from other companies. Hahn and Noll estimate that the utility would receive 28 percent and 31 percent of the initial permits based upon pre-control and current standards, respectively, but would require 44 percent under the competitive result. To achieve the competitive result, the utility may account for all purchases of permits—all other firms would be sellers—and thus would face strong incentives to engage in monopsonistic purchasing practices.

To overcome these unfortunate side effects of the distribution formulas, Hahn and Noll suggest several alternative modifications in the administration of the permit system. One possibility is to allocate to the potential monopsonist the amount of permits that equals the estimated competitive result and use the historical basis for allocating permits to other firms. This scheme would avoid monopsony while providing incentives for others to trade, thereby generating a competitive outcome. Another scheme would be to allocate only part of the permits and have the state auction off the remainder. While the auction generates revenues—and thus creates potential losers—the efficiency gains to industry from rationalizing abatement may offset the revenue loss.

The most ingenious approach Hahn and Noll propose to achieve political feasibility and economic efficiency is a "zero-revenue auction" in which each firm receives an initial allocation, but is then required to offer its entire allocation for sale in the auction. Each firm reports its demand curve for permits, and the aggregate demand curve determines the market-clearing price. Using an auction mechanism rather than waiting for normal market forces to cause trades has two efficiency advantages: placing all firms on the same side of the market avoids the exercise of monopoly power, and having all firms participate in the establishment of the market price maximizes the amount of information conveyed by the initial permit price. This auction avoids the political problem of revenue generation, since the gross payments firms make to the state are counterbalanced by the gross payments the states makes to firms based on the initial allocation. Indeed, the scheme would not harm any existing polluter, since any firm could maintain the status quo by reporting a perfectly inelastic demand curve—its post-auction allocation would equal its pre-auction allocation, and thus the firm would make zero net payments to the system.[15]

CONCLUDING REMARKS

The United States now spends almost $40 billion per year on environmental protection requirements, or about 1.5 percent of its gross national product. Modifying regulatory requirements to encourage more cost-effective and cost-beneficial results could reduce the bill, while allowing the same or greater environmental progress. The increasing focus on regulatory reform suggests that these economics-based proposals will receive more serious consideration than in the past. The recent release of several detailed case studies of how such policies would actually work—as well as EPA's growing experience with its bubble and other controlled trading programs—will add empirical flesh to the strong a priori case for economics-based programs.

Proponents of economics-based reforms must do more than reiterate or quantify the efficiency advantages of these policies. They must acknowledge and confront the political problems that arise because some groups stand to lose from reform. Other groups, such as those with high compliance costs, will gain in the switch to economic criteria and may well support the change. If regulatory reform is like other reforms, though, those who wish to modify the system will have to demonstrate that the changes are fair.

Brief analysis of the current regulatory system indicates that Congress and EPA created a large number of accommodations to potential losers when the system originally changed from very modest to stringent environmental controls. Indeed, these accommodations—use of affordability criteria, stricter controls on new rather than existing sources, and tax incentives and municipal public works projects—explain the characteristics of the system that economists and other analysts seek to reform.

This chapter identifies the likely losers, and the severity of their losses under various economic-based reforms. The analysis demonstrates that the potential severity of losses increases along with the likely efficiency gains as one progresses from current EPA reforms to cost-effectiveness tests, to cost-benefit tests, and finally to economic incentive schemes. Economic incentive schemes can, in fact, generate enormous transfers from polluters (and their customers and workers) to the government treasury, transfers that may well outnumber the cost savings to polluters from removing inflexible command-and-control regulations.

Losers from regulatory reforms can be accommodated so that efficiency-enhancing changes can take place. Some accommodations to political feasibility may, however, compromise the efficiency of the reforms. Indeed, conflicts between efficiency and political notions of equity are likely to be common in translating the concept of reform into practical institutions. Designing institutions that simultaneously achieve equity, efficiency and political feasibility should be a priority for both researchers and government officials interested in reform of environmental regulation.

NOTES

1. For a classic statement of the reasons for these economics-based reforms, see Schultze (1977). See also Anderson et al. (1977). For a recent study of the strengths and weaknesses of economic incentive schemes, see Schelling et al. (forthcoming).

2. For a discussion of the possible bases of regulatory standard setting, see Lave (1981).

3. For a more detailed discussion of this particular case and of the problems with compensation in general, see Goldfarb (1980).

4. Note, however, that this compensation is after the fact. That is, deregulation of trucking routes had been largely accomplished via administrative action; it was not necessary to compensate firms in this way to accomplish this reform. The Reagan Administration may have felt that the future of deregulation in trucking depended on providing compensation to firms, but this is pure speculation.

5. Critics, however, have pointed out many flaws in the construction grant program (Harrison and Leone, forthcoming).

6. The savings from using tax-exempt bonds to finance pollution control were approximately $120 million in 1979 (Lulkovich 1981), compared to total expenditures on air and water pollution control of $37 billion (Council on Environmental Quality 1981).

7. Letter from Douglas M. Costle to Ray Marshall, July 6, 1979.

8. Cost-effectiveness tests may reduce the demand for goods and services other than pollution control equipment. For example, Eastern coal interests would lose along with scrubber manufacturers if EPA eliminated the percentage requirement on sulfur oxide standards discussed previously.

9. Information on the wastewater characteristics of pulp and paper plants is taken from Meta Systems, Inc. (1980).

10. The BCT example is not a simple cost-effectiveness test, since the overall level of control was reduced (at least in theory) when BCT was substituted for BAT standards for conventional pollutants. Indeed, even some pulp and paper firms may find their costs reduced with the BCT guidelines. Environmentalists may oppose cost-effectiveness tests partly because they suspect such tests would be combined with some reduction in the stringency of standards, as in the BCT example.

11. The estimates of costs and benefits for control of benzene from maleic anhydride plants are taken from Harrison (1981). Additional information is contained in Nichols (forthcoming).

12. The section, "Accommodations to Losers from Reforms," discusses the possibilities of modifying the revenues generated by the economic incentive schemes.

13.   Industries likely to bear the largest costs have large precontrol pollution levels, high control costs, and markets that face stiff outside competition and in which demand is elastic.
14.   The discussion in this section relies upon Palmer and Quinn (1981).
15.   It will generally not be efficient for a firm to maintain the status quo, since the firm would usually gain from participating in the auction. We wish to thank Roger Noll for pointing out the equity advantages of the zero-revenue auction from the standpoint of an individual firm, as well as for other suggestions regarding our discussion of marketable permits.

REFERENCES

Ackerman, Bruce, and William Hassler. 1981. *Clean Coal/Dirty Air*. New Haven: Yale University Press.

Anderson, Frederick R.; Allen V. Kneese; Phillip D. Reed; Serge Taylor; and Russell B. Stevenson. 1977. *Environmental Improvement through Economic Incentives*. Baltimore: Johns Hopkins Press.

Anderson, Robert, Jr.; Robert O. Reid; and Eugene P. Seskin. 1979. "An Analysis of Alternative Policies for Attainment and Maintenance of a Short-term NO₂ Standard." Princeton: Mathtech (September 17).

Baumol, William J., and Wallace E. Oates. 1979. *Economics, Environmental Policy, and the Quality of Life*. Englewood Cliffs, N.J.: Prentice-Hall.

Clark, Timothy B. 1979. "New Approaches to Regulatory Reform—Letting the Market Do the Job." *National Journal* 11, no. 32 (August 11):1316–22.

Council on Environmental Quality. 1981. *Environmental Quality: 1980*. 11th Annual Report. Washington, D.C.: Government Printing Office.

David, Martin; Wayland Eheart; Erhard Joeres; and Elizabeth David. 1977. "Marketable Effluent Permits for the Control of Phosphorous Effluent in Lake Michigan." Social Systems Research Institute Working Paper. University of Wisconsin (December).

Environmental Protection Agency. 1981. "The Incremental Cost-Effectiveness of Selected EPA Regulations." Draft Report (January 23).

Goldfarb, Robert S. 1980. "Compensating the Victims of Policy Change." *Regulation* 4, no. 5 (September/October): 22–30.

Harrison, David, Jr. 1981. "Cost-Benefit Principles and the Regulation of Environmental Carcinogens." In *Management of Assessed Risk for Carcinogens*, edited by William J. Nicholson, pp. 109–22. New York: New York Academy of Sciences.

Harrison, David, Jr. Forthcoming. "Charges, Marketable Permits, and Other Mechanisms for the Regulation of Aircraft Noise." In *Incentive Arrangements for Environmental Protection: A Critical Examination*, Thomas Schelling et al. Cambridge, Mass.: MIT Press.

Harrison, David, Jr., and Robert A. Leone. Forthcoming. *Federal Water Pollution Control Policy*. Washington, D.C.: The American Enterprise Institute.

Harrison, David, Jr., and Paul R. Portney. 1981. "Making Ready for the Clean Air Act." *Regulation* 5, no. 2 (March/April): 24–31.

Harrison, David, Jr., and Paul R. Portney. Forthcoming. "Regulatory Reform in the Large and the Small." In *Reforming the New Social Regulation*, edited by LeRoy Graymer. Beverly Hills: Sage Publications.

Kelman, Stephen J. 1981. "Economists and the Environmental Muddle." *Public Interest*, no. 64 (Summer): 106–23.

Kneese, Allen V., and Charles L. Schultze. 1975. *Pollution, Prices and Public Policy*. Washington, D.C.: Brookings Institution.

Lave, Lester. 1981. *The Strategy of Social Regulation*. Washington, D.C.: Brookings Institution.

Leone, Robert A., and John E. Jackson. 1981. "The Political Economy of Federal Regulatory Activity." In *Studies in Public Regulation*, edited by G. Fromm. Cambridge, Mass.: MIT Press.

Lulkovich, Joan. 1981. "Tax-Exempt Volume Hits $46.28 Billion a Year, Topping Previous Record in '78." *Weekly Bond Buyer* (January 12).

Meta Systems, Inc. 1980. *Economic Impact of Water Effluent Guidelines on the Pulp and Paper Industry*. Cambridge, Mass. (April).

Nichols, Albert. Forthcoming. "Alternative Strategies for Regulating Airborne Benzene." In *Incentive Arrangements for Environmental Protection: A Critical Examination*, Thomas Schelling et al. Cambridge, Mass.: MIT Press.

Palmer, Adele R.; William E. Mooz; Timothy H. Quinn; and Kathleen A. Wolf. 1980. "Economic Implications of Regulating Chlorofluorocarbon Emissions from Nonaerosol Applications." Report R-2524-EPA. Santa Monica: Rand Corporation (June).

Palmer, Adele R., and Timothy H. Quinn. 1981. "Allocating Chlorofluorocarbon Permits: Who Gains, Who Loses, and What Is the Cost?" Report R-2806-EPA. Santa Monica: Rand Corporation (July).

Schelling, Thomas, C.; David Harrison, Jr.; Steven J. Kelman; Albert L. Nichols; and Robert Repetto. Forthcoming. *Incentive Arrangements for Environmental Protection: A Critical Examination*. Cambridge, Mass.: MIT Press.

Schultze, Charles L. 1977. *The Public Use of Private Interest*. Washington, D.C.: Brookings Institution.

Seskin, Eugene. 1978. "Automobile Air Pollution Policy." In *Current Issues in U.S. Environmental Policy*, edited by Paul R. Portney, pp. 68–104. Baltimore: Johns Hopkins Press.

White, Lawrence, J. 1981. *Reforming Regulation: Processes and Problems*. Englewood Cliffs, N.J.: Prentice-Hall.

INDEX

181

ABOUT THE EDITOR

Wesley A. Magat is past director of the Center for the Study of Business Regulation in Duke University's Fuqua School of Business, and holds a joint appointment in the Institute of Policy Sciences and Public Affairs. He organized and chaired the Regulation Center's Conference on Reform of Environmental Regulation in May, 1981, for which the chapters in this volume were commissioned. He received his Ph.D. in managerial economics and decision sciences from Northwestern University and has worked as consultant for several organizations on problems of government regulation. His primary research interest is in problems of regulation, particularly environmental regulation. His past work has examined rulemaking in social regulatory agencies and the effects of environmental regulation on innovation.

LIST OF
CONTRIBUTORS

Robert Dorfman, D.A. Wells Professor of Political Economy, Harvard University, Cambridge, Massachusetts

James H. Ware, Associate Professor of Biostatistics, Harvard School of Public Health, Harvard University, Boston, Massachusetts

A. Myrick Freeman III, Professor of Economics, Bowdoin College, Brunswick, Maine

James W. Vaupel, Associate Professor of Public Policy and Business, Duke University, Durham, North Carolina

Marc J. Roberts, Professor of Political Economy and Health Policy, Harvard School of Public Health, Boston, Massachusetts

Robert W. Hahn, Research Economist, California Institute of Technology, Pasadena, California

Roger G. Noll, Professor of Economics and Chairman of Division of the Humanities and Social Sciences, California Institute of Technology, Pasadena, California

David Harrison, Jr., Associate Professor, John F. Kennedy School of Government, Harvard University, Cambridge, Massachusetts.

Paul R. Portney, Senior Fellow, Resources for the Future